D1220937

WHEN I DO, I LEARN

WHEN I DO, I LEARN

A Guide to
Creative Planning
for Teachers and Parents of
Preschool Children

Barbara J. Taylor

Brigham Young University Press, Provo, Utah

Other books by the author:

A Child Goes Forth
I Can Do

International Standard Book Number: 0-8425-0954-2
Library of Congress Catalog Card Number: 74-2122
© 1974 by Brigham Young University Press. All rights reserved
Printed in the United States of America
Brigham Young University Press, Provo, Utah 84602
1974 5M 0322

LIBRARY OF CONGRESS CATALOGING IN PUBLICATION DATA.

Taylor, Barbara J.
When I do, I learn.

Bibliography: p.
1.   Education, Preschool.   2.   Creative activities
and seat work.   I.   Title.
LB1140.2.T29   372.1'3   74-2122
ISBN O-8425-0954-2

When I hear, I forget.
When I see, I remember.
When I do, I learn.
—An Old Chinese Proverb

CONTENTS

PREFACE

Anyone can provide time-consuming activities to keep a child busy, but one must have considerable skill and knowledge in order to provide activities which will help the child develop socially, physically, emotionally, and cognitively. *When I Do, I Learn* has been written for the professional teacher, the undergraduate student, the lay teacher, the parent, and anyone else who is responsible for providing and coordinating educational activities that will help the preschool child develop self-confidence, independence, and creative freedom.

The book is a guide—not a cut-and-dried how-to-do-it book. It contains numerous simple-to-apply ideas that can be used in a group or in a home setting. Experiences with everyday ideas and materials help the child understand and appreciate his world. Extravagant, expensive approaches have less meaning for him. If an adult is told exactly *how* to teach a child and *why*, his initiative in executing ideas is destroyed or, at best, limited. But if the adult is given examples of how different aspects of the environment can be incorporated into good learning activities for children, he can then feel comfortable as he tries out his own ideas.

No time limit is suggested for the various activities outlined in the book; the child you teach should determine this. As long as he is interested, let him explore. When he begins to get bored, help him shift to another activity. Use the clock for more important things—for getting somewhere on time or for boiling a two-minute egg. Learn to recognize the value and excitement of utilizing spontaneous, natural events. Perhaps you have planned to plant seeds and your child discovers a bird with a broken wing. You should be able to shift your attention to the wounded animal and plan to plant seeds later. It is seldom that you will have the same firsthand experience with a bird. Besides, the child is already very interested in the bird.

Of course, if you just sit back and wait for such spontaneous events to happen all of the time, you will be disappointed. It is wise to plan for all kinds of experiences—as long as they have meaning for the child. Make them as realistic as possible, using the very best available aids and methods. Then when a spontaneous event comes along to support this teaching, it will reinforce the child's understanding of his world rather than merely confuse him.

As you select ideas to teach your preschooler, be very observant—listen to his conversation, observe his actions and interactions, determine his interests and concerns. If you want to know what and how much your child learns, first find out what he already knows, second introduce him to an activity, then determine how his knowledge has increased. With a preschooler, you can determine this from evaluating his actions and language. Your objectives and evaluation must be flexible enough so that no matter where the child currently is in his learning, he will be able to grow because of the activities provided. Rigid criteria for performance creates tension between the one who is doing the teaching and the one who is doing the learning. Perhaps you over- or under-plan, or perhaps the child is frustrated or bored. A lack of interest might even exist on the part of the child and/or the teacher. You can evaluate the child's progress by being keenly observant without requiring him to give some kind of stereotyped performance.

Several behavioral objectives are provided in each chapter and many more could easily be added; but the intent of the book is to acquaint the adult with objectives that the child can achieve with each topic. You shouldn't try to teach all of these objectives, but rather select only those that are appropriate or design others which can be more beneficial to the child.

Many of the ideas in the book may appear to be useful in only the ideal situation—the type of situation often found in university nursery schools. However, there are numerous ideas which are suited for use in any home or in any nursery school setting, whether it be the state-owned or the private school which operates within the bounds of prohibitive laws. All you need do is adapt ideas and approaches to your particular circumstances, focusing always on the needs and interests of the children involved.

This book is designed to meet the needs of many different people. The trend is now moving away from some government educational programs toward teaching children in the home. But many parents lack the knowledge or expertise to attack this job even though they greatly desire to do so. This book can be a valuable aid to them in planning home experiences. Stress is placed on those things which are most important to young children—the ones in their everyday lives—and these are fun for both parent and child to share.

Another current movement is the introduction of many day-care or child-care centers. Rather than seek those which provide strictly custodial care, you more than likely will desire those which provide educational programs. If you are a teacher in one of these centers, you should find this book highly valuable.

No matter how much or how little experience teachers of preschool children have had, most are always alert to new or different ways of presenting material, for they recognize the value of change and flexibility in the learning process. This book provides many stimulating possibilities for the teacher, the child, and the parent who have the desire and the courage to be innovative.

Because of the convenience of conventional usage, I have occasionally used masculine pronouns when I have referred to the child, the parent, and the teacher. I am not inferring in any way that the masculine role is the primary one; both male and female figures are, of course, indispensible in the training of preschoolers.

I have included wherever possible all publishing information for each book I have listed; in several cases, however, such information was not available.

I am grateful to the following for their help and cooperation: the Brigham Young University Child Development Laboratories and the Salt Lake City Community Action Center for letting us photograph their various nursery school activities; Karen Silva for her work on the production phase of the book; Julie Fuhriman, artist; Stan Macbean, photographer; McRay Magleby, Jr., designer; and Kerril Sue Rollins, editor.

WHY A WRITTEN LESSON PLAN? 1

Suppose you are going to Europe—a trip you have dreamed about for so long that it has almost seemed real. You eagerly start planning, realizing that if you continue to dream, waiting for details to miraculously fall into place, you will never make it to the airport, let alone across the ocean.

First of all, you check airline reservations, time schedules, costs, how much luggage can be taken without extra charge. You also check accommodations in both the United States and Europe: How much are they? What does the cost include or exclude? How will you change your money into the currency of different countries? Will the food agree with you? How will you make yourself understood in France, Spain, Germany? You also consider where to apply for a passport, how long it takes to get one, whether shots are required, and what will happen to things at home, such as plants and mail. The list runs on and on. If you tackle and solve it at the outset, your trip will be pleasureable and leisurely—if you do not, you will be frustrated and unhappy.

If you are going to Europe the easy way—on a tour which takes care of all transportation, accommodations, and other details—you still need to plan for your own personal needs: proper clothing, adequate money, cosmetics, to name only a few. Good planning doesn't just happen; it takes effort and results in a happy, successful vacation.

The same principle applies when you teach preschool children—helping them discover the simple and intricate wonders of their world—whether you are a professional, a nonprofessional, or a parent. Good planning results in a classroom atmosphere that encourages maximum learning, and successful teachers have found that it is done best with a written lesson plan—a detailed agenda for each day which has one major theme with behavioral objectives for the preschoolers to achieve and the supporting activities which allow them to realize these objectives. Successful learning consists of three things: knowing where you're going, how to get there, and when you've arrived (Mager, 1968). A written lesson plan helps you and the children do just that.

WHY WRITTEN PLANS FOR YOUNG CHILDREN

It is wise to use a written lesson plan for several reasons:

- You must think through what is to be taught. You are often the only one who knows what must be planned for. And if you cannot be with the children at a particular time, someone else can carry out the daily schedule of events as outlined on your written plan.
- Written lesson plans can be shared with parents as well. If a copy of each plan is posted where it draws the parent's attention, it will most likely be read and appreciated. And then the learning card (discussed later), which each child brings home, means more to his parents.
- One exposure to a topic is not enough for young children—they learn through repetition. As you introduce a topic to them a second, a third, or a fourth time, they can review what they have learned previously and then step further into the topic. They are also able to relate the topic to other aspects of their environment. This type of review also helps the teacher.
- Such a lesson plan, rather than causing rigidity, allows both you and the children more freedom: (1) You are able to see that you can outline various routes to the desired goals. You can also be flexible in scheduling activities, for you see that you can allow for group interaction, individual pursuit, active and quiet play. These important items are sometimes more visible on paper than in actual practice. (2) Finally, when you have scheduled all necessary activities, you are able to discern whether sufficient time has been allotted for the children to thoroughly explore the materials or activities. If not, you can then decide with relative ease which other activities can be shortened or eliminated as part of the whole school day, as you are prompted by the interests of the children. Children probably learn more from "messing around" than they do from conforming to structure all of the time. They also learn "independently, not in bunches; . . . they learn out of interest and curiosity, not to please or appease the adults in power; . . . they ought to be in control of their own learning" (Holt, 1967:153).

ITEMS FOR CONSIDERATION

First of all, you must decide what you want to teach. Then upon selection of a topic, answer a number of questions:

- Why do I want to teach this particular topic to young children? Will it help them lay a foundation for later learning, or could it best be saved for later when they have more language skills and personal experiences? "Intentional learning is more efficient than incidental learning" (Landreth, 1972:9).

- If the topic is appropriate, what will I need in order to teach it? What kinds of visual aids will best support the experience? (It is important to select the very best aids available.)

- How will I teach it? Is there a time of day or week which is best for this particular experience? How much time should I allow? Is this the most effective way to teach this topic?

- Are there some new terms to introduce and define? If so, how will I make sure the children understand their proper use? Are there some experiences I should design so that I can see the children putting into practice some of the new terms or ideas?

- Am I teaching truth? When young children are learning new things, they need to have accurate information. For instance, having human characteristics applied to animals and inanimate objects only confuses them. After they acquire the ability to relate to all different aspects of their world, and develop the ability to think abstractly, they will be more able to tolerate ambiguities. For now, they need realistic first-hand experiences.

- Are the concepts on the developmental level of the children? Occasionally, a review of abilities of children at different age levels is helpful. Planning beyond their developmental level results in frustration for them; planning below it results in boredom. It is important that you plan experiences which will be of interest to the children and which will challenge and stimulate them. "Any subject can be taught effectively in some intellectually honest form to any child at any stage of development." The task is "one of presenting the structure of that subject in terms of the child's way of viewing things" (Bruner, 1960:33).

- What is the composition of the group? Are the children of similar age and background? If so, the planning will be easier even though few children are on exactly the same developmental level in all areas. If not, you will have to provide experiences and information for different developmental levels. Chronological age is not the best criteria for planning; individual children as well as the entire make-up of the group must be considered.

- Is variety necessary? Yes. You should provide for it in the themes that you introduce and in daily activities, gearing it to the interests and needs of the children. It is very important, however, that ideas or themes be repeated periodically so that the children will have more than one exposure from which to form concepts. But if everything in the lesson plan is geared to the theme, the children may become bored. Activities should be selected which will best add knowledge about the theme.

- When is the optimum time for learning? When interested, the child learns faster and has better retention. It may be necessary for you to stimulate

learning in certain areas or it may be that a child will inquire about something. The *teachable moments* are priceless. You may plan a particular topic for one day, but then something exciting happens: Helen brings her mother cat and kittens, or Sam finds a cocoon in a nearby tree. A wise teacher will be flexible enough to go along with the interests of the children that day or as soon as possible if special outside preparation is necessary. When we are really interested in something, we can be sustained in it for a long period of time; and we don't want anyone trying to divert us. A few statistics on vocabulary, academic skills, and intelligence point out the important relationship between a child's early years and his learning ability:

By age six, children have 50 percent of the vocabulary they will have at age eight and at age eight have 50 percent of the vocabulary they will have by age eighteen. Regarding academic skills (vocabulary development, reading comprehension, and general school achievement) that children have obtained at age eighteen, 33 percent develops between birth and age six, with 42 percent coming between ages six and thirteen, and 25 percent between ages

4

thirteen and eighteen. As measured at age seventeen, 50 percent of intellectual development occurs between conception and age four, about 30 percent between ages four and eight, and about 20 percent between ages eight and seventeen (Bloom, 1964).

- Which area of the child's development should be most emphasized? A lesson plan should include activities which allow the child to develop physically, socially, emotionally, spiritually, and intellectually. You must carefully plan each day so that all of these are provided for.

HOW TO MAKE A WRITTEN LESSON PLAN

Teachers and the parents of young children have a great deal of influence on whether they have happy, successful experiences. That is why you must plan carefully the experiences over which you have control. Their time with you should be as exciting as your trip to Europe! Actually, you begin with the *end* in mind—what you hope the children will be able to do or say as a result of a specific experience—and your lesson plan flows from that point.

5

Daily Lesson Plan

_____   _____

(School or teacher's name)   (Date)

Daily Lesson Plan

THEME: The subject matter of the day.

PREASSESSMENT: Finding out what is known about the theme.

CONCEPTS: Specific truths to be taught.

BEHAVIORAL OBJECTIVES: What you expect the children to do or say as a result of this experience.

LEARNING ACTIVITIES: The activities you provide to help the children accomplish the behavioral objectives.

SCHEDULE OF ACTIVITIES:
Review plans for the day
Check-in
Setting the learning stage
Free play
    Housekeeping area
    Food experience
    Blocks—large and small
    Creative expression
    Manipulative area
    Cognitive, sensory, and/or science area
    Book corner and books
Prestory activities
Story time
Music
Snack or lunch
Outside activities
Check-out

LEARNING CARD: Providing information and follow-through for parents.

EVALUATION: Summarizing strengths and weaknesses of the plan and the day.

PLAN FOR TOMORROW: Focusing on the goals you hope to accomplish in short- and long-range planning for individual children as well as for the group.

BOOKS AVAILABLE THROUGHOUT THE DAY: A list of books which support the daily theme or provide appropriate diversion.

Identification

The name of the school or teacher, as well as the date, should appear on each lesson plan. By knowing exactly when specific information was presented, you can provide a better evaluation of the child's progress, interests, and knowledge. You can also repeat certain topics more successfully by placing them at appropriate intervals.

The lesson plan is a guide for teaching, allowing for flexibility. For additional help in writing a lesson plan or for different ideas on the various curriculum areas, see *A Child Goes Forth* by Barbara J. Taylor.

Theme

Some teachers prefer to teach without gearing their ideas or materials to a specific theme because they feel a theme limits their focus. They want the children to be the ones who decide the curriculum. In some cases this is good, but in other cases when little or no direction exists, the children suffer from lack of adult guidance.

If you find it difficult to decide upon a theme, here is a valuable hint. Listen carefully to your children and watch them. You will be amazed at the multitude of ideas they can give you, ideas which will help them learn more about themselves and their environment.

The theme is the subject matter of the day, but it may also be a part of a larger unit.

Preassessment

Before attempting to teach any topic, you must find out just what the children know about it. Without this information you will not know where to start. Advanced material causes frustration and material already known causes lack of interest.

Preassessment is to be done prior to any teaching of the topic. It can be done in a formal, organized manner or it can be of a casual nature. Just talking informally with a child about a certain topic can help you evaluate how much knowledge the child has, what his interests are, if his information is accurate, and if additional exposure would be of value to him. Socrates directed the thinking of his students almost entirely by questions. This type of teaching is becoming popular again. You ask instead of tell.

The child's existing knowledge forms the basis for a lesson plan. You may also need to do additional research into the subject area, and may have considered an approach entirely different from that indicated by the preassessment. You may also realize that the topic is so broad that it will take several days to present rather than just one. Preassessment, then, guides you to appropriate, meaningful planning.

Concepts

Concepts are simple, short statements which convey the specific truths you intend to teach. The number of concepts used in one lesson plan varies depending on the theme, how much information is to be imparted for the day, and whatever is needed to help the children understand the ideas presented.

If you introduce new terms or ideas, be sure to provide experiences or definitions which will make them meaningful to the children. Just learning to say a new word or idea is not sufficient; each child must have the opportunity to use it in a practical way—only then does it become worthwhile to him.

Behavioral Objectives

Beginning with the *end* in mind, you immediately think about behavioral objectives, a means of evaluating whether the child has learned the material. They are stated in such a way that almost anyone can judge from the performance of each child whether his behavior in word or action demonstrates his mastery or lack of mastery.

Behavioral objectives state under what conditions each child will be able to perform (at the end of the unit, when supplied certain experiences) and specifically what he will be able to say or do as a result of the particular experience. They are simply stated and performance is easily observed.

The number of behavioral objectives is dictated by the particular children involved and the complexity of the theme. You may have just one behavioral objective or you may have any number. Some may even be subobjectives. If you have preassessed accurately and planned well, the children will be able to accomplish the objectives you set.

Learning Activities

This is merely a summarized list of the activities provided during the day which help the children accomplish the behavioral objectives. These activities can be treated and enhanced in a variety of ways, depending on the theme of each lesson plan and the behavioral objective(s).

Schedule of Activities

Review Plans for the Day

Before the children arrive, you should take time to sit down with other teachers to review the daily plan. Assignments can be made and each person can review his responsibilities for the entire day. This meeting solidifies the daily plan and helps you run the day's activities in a smooth manner. You should have the children clean up their areas before they move on to other activities.

Also you, or another teacher, should be ready to begin each activity as the first child arrives in your area. Each area of the curriculum is considered and provided for, but the sequence of activities can be arranged in whatever manner best suits the individual group. It is strongly recommended, however, that the first activity after the children arrive be Setting the Learning Stage, for it is here that the entire tone of the day is laid. This activity helps the children center their thinking on the theme; as a result, the supporting activities throughout have more meaning. You should be flexible and feel free to lengthen, shorten, or eliminate activities, according to the interests of the children. Planning for all areas in the curriculum is necessary, but you should never feel obligated to use all of them just because you planned for them.

Information for each activity is included in some detail in the lesson plan. Listing just the name of the activity is insufficient. You should record specifically what you have planned for each area of the curriculum, as listed here:

Check-in

This involves listing what materials the children can use while they wait for other children to arrive and also any special information to be imparted to them.

Setting the learning stage

You call all the children together and explain the format for the day, introducing the basic concepts and channeling the children's thinking toward the theme. This activity occurs daily.

Free play

In this activity the children are free to select materials and activities of their choice and are permitted to use them for the duration of their interest. They are not required to go to all areas nor are they limited in the amount of time they spend in one area. Some free-play activities are:

- Housekeeping area: specific props or information is used in this area during the day. Some days require more activities than others. Some type of dramatic play should be provided daily although it may not be emphasized.
- Food experience: most often it is better, when a food experience is used, to have it near the beginning of the day so that the food can be eaten during snack or lunch. Some foods require lengthy preparation and/or cooking, and unless they are made soon after the children arrive, they will not be ready for that day.

    A food experience is not required each day, but sometimes it supports the theme so well that it is a must. Other times, food is not appropriate or desired. But, needless to say, children do enjoy it.

- Blocks (large and small): because block play encourages physical development, social development, problem solving, cooperation, and use of language (to mention only a few), children should be exposed daily to such activity. There may be more activity with some themes than others, but if the teacher provides for it, the children will decide whether they will use it.
- Creative expression: here is another daily must (only rare occasions will eliminate it, such as a long field trip or better ways to support the theme). Children need raw materials and a lot of time to express themselves. This is an art period which encourages creativity, use of small muscles, sharing of materials, and which gives the children something to talk about.

  Sometimes it is very difficult to think of an art project that will support a given theme. But instead of worrying about it, you need provide only some materials and opportunities for the children to explore, letting them enjoy the experience. Products are less important to young children than processes.
- Manipulative area: because small muscles develop more slowly than large muscles, young children need opportunities to exercise these small ones.

Even children who are easily frustrated with small muscle activities will find satisfaction in making objects if the activity looks interesting. Frequent exposure to manipulative toys encourages their use.

- Cognitive, sensory, and/or science area: most centers have an area or table devoted to stimulating the interests of the children. This is a good way for you to preassess a theme for a later date. Put the materials out on the table and let the children explore them, then both the children and you can ask and answer questions.

  Some days you will find that cognitive items fit more closely into the theme; on other days sensory or science items are more appropriate. If you want to help the children more fully understand their environment, place objects or materials in this area which will stimulate their curiosity, require problem solving, and encourage verbalization. The kinds of materials and/or activities placed here should be varied so that each child will be interested in those which are new and different.

- Book corner and books: books should be available daily in a quiet, relaxed place for individual browsing by the children or for small group stories. The preschoolers should be encouraged to use books, for they discover many pleasures from looking at them or hearing stories from them. You can also help them discover new information from such sources.

  Books provided may support the daily theme or be some favorites of the children. Periodic rotation of the books will stimulate interest.

Prestory activities

- Actually the activities used here could be used at any time, not just before a story. Perhaps they could better be called transition activities. At any rate, their main function is to bring the children into a group in preparation for the next activity—in this case, a story. If the children are really interested, they will be ready and eager to participate.

  Rather than use one kind of activity each day (a fingerplay or song for instance), you can introduce a variety of ideas. "Why hurry to always do the same fingerplay?"—which the child might not like anyway—could easily be changed to "I want to get there because I don't want to miss anything." You can help determine the attitude of the children by what you provide and also by your attitude.

Story time

This occurs almost every day, but there are some occasions when this time can be more meaningfully used, such as when there is a guest, a field trip, or some other extra activity. It is important for children to hear language and to learn to listen. Stories provide delightful enjoyment and information for them.

As it isn't always possible to find a story which supports the daily theme, feel free to use one that will appeal to the group. When a story does fit the theme, it is well to use it to restate some of the daily concepts.

Let the children decide how many stories they hear. Plan several if the interest of the children is high, but feel comfortable in using just one story (even in shortened form) if that is what the children want. If some children want to hear the same story over ("Tell it again, teacher"), have those who want to hear it again stay and let those go who are ready for the next activity.

Use a variety of stories (in content) and present them in different and interesting ways (use of book, flannel board, flip-card, real objects, puppets).

Story time should involve all of the children together, but don't hesitate to encourage children to look at books or to listen to stories in a small group or individually during the day. Select books that are realistic in concepts and in illustrations. As well as being enjoyable, story time is an excellent teaching time.

Music

Music can also "soothe the savage beast" in children, helping them relax and express themselves. Even though music is listed as a separate period here, it should be encouraged throughout the day—as children are interacting with materials and activities, for quieting the children for story time or another group activity, for relaxation at the snack, for active participation outside.

Music can also change the pace of the children. If they are listless and disinterested, play a lively record or rhythm on the piano. If they are rowdy and aggressive, try the soothing effects of a quiet or slow rhythm.

Music is more than just singing. It is also finding rhythm in our everyday lives—the movement of animals, the swaying of trees in the breeze, the whirring of a fan or motor, the song of a bird.

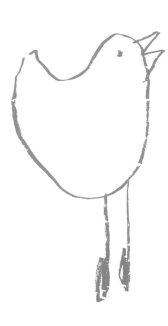

Provide some experiences where the children can demonstrate their ideas and feelings about the things around them—the patter of the rain, the definite beat of a drum, the slow, steady step of the elephant. All of these experiences belong in the repertoire of a young child, and the teacher can provide them for him at any time of the day.

Invite guests in to show children how various instruments are played, the names of the parts, the kind of instrument. Most of the children won't be able to play these instruments, but they enjoy seeing them and learning about their unique qualities.

Play records of classical music and call them by name. Soon some of the children will ask for one of these records by name, and you will be thrilled that they are now aware that each of the records has its own name.

You might feel more inadequate in the use of music with young children than in any other area of the curriculum, but you should continually use music—either by introducing it yourself or having an enthusiastic qualified person do it. If you eliminate it (or use it only minimally), you rob the children of a very important experience.

Snack or lunch

This seems to be one of the best social times of the entire day. Children who leisurely eat their food and share their ideas with others while relaxing gain the most from this activity. Their conversation may center around the theme of the day or it may involve something exciting in a child's life.

If you are seated at the table with the children, you can supply necessary items at appropriate times (more food, a sponge, answers to questions). When you stay seated, so do the children.

The children should be encouraged to dominate the conversation, serve themselves, and remove their dishes and utensils after eating. They enjoy developing independence.

Some children may even be asked to help set the table and/or serve the food. This is often an experience they don't have at home. Low tables and equipment of appropriate size generally allow them to do a pretty good job. However, if this takes them away from a more beneficial activity, you may want to have another teacher prepare the tables.

Outside Activities

This is a must, even if the weather is bad. Children need the fresh air and exercise which the outdoors provides. Even a short stay refreshes each child and helps him release some of his energy in a manner not acceptable inside the building.

Equipment need not be elaborate. Raw materials such as boards and boxes can be used in endless ways limited only by the creativity of the children and teachers. Concepts are sometimes best supported by activities enjoyed outside.

If children are outside when their parents come to get them, it is usually easier to get them away from the school than when they are inside with so many tantalizing things to delay departure.

Check-out

As it nears time to go home, the children should be encouraged to return equipment to its proper place. A parent is usually patient enough to allow the child time to put away his toys, but you may need to give him a small reminder. Each child can then learn that not only is it fun to get things out, it can be just as fun to see them back in their proper places.

Upon departure, each child is given a learning card (discussed below). Children in the habit of receiving these cards often won't go home without one. It

is sometimes necessary to explain that there are days when they won't get them and that they can tell their parents about the things they have done that day.

Learning Card

Because of the constant request of parents to know what their children do at school, the learning card was designed. This also has reduced the pressure on the child to daily answer his parents' inevitable question—"What did you do today?" Now it becomes more of a sharing time with results, both parent and child answering and asking questions in a casual relaxed atmosphere.

A learning card is an informal overview of the day, explaining the activities and concepts presented and is in no way meant to be an instrument for interrogation by the parents. Nor does it indicate a level of performance by which the child should be judged. Rather, it is designed to provide a common frame of reference for informal discussion between the child and his parents. The child may talk about something interesting that happened at school and the parent can then support the conversation because of the information written on the card. Or, after seeing a learning card, a parent might say, "Oh, at school today

14

you had a fireman come to visit." The child then usually picks up the conversation with excitement and shares his experiences.

The learning card is also a tool by which you can assess whether the child has mastered information correctly from the feedback supplied by the parents. Here again, the card is used for a tie between parents and teachers. Either one could initiate a comment or question. The learning card, prepared for each change of theme, may cover a day, a week, or a unit.

Keeping the size of the learning card constant, such as a 3" x 5" index card, encourages parents to file it for future reference. Elaborate cards take teaching time and are unnecessary—you should convey basic information to parents rather than display artistic prowess. Tell the parents the cards will be coming home, and they will look forward to and plan for them.

Evaluation

The evaluation of the lesson plan occurs after the children have gone home, but it is wise to design some specific questions as you prepare the plan in order to determine if the children have learned the concepts. You may want your staff to be aware of certain children, certain activities, or particular times during the day. If you call these things to their attention as you go over the plan for that day, evaluation will be easier.

Design some pointed questions or comments to begin the evaluation period, which generally takes from fifteen to sixty minutes, depending upon items to be discussed and the availability of time for staff members. If other items come up which are more important than the ones designed, focus attention on them. Aim for the best use of the evaluation time. Here are a few suggestions:

- Which children seem to feel the most self-confident as they express themselves verbally and/or physically?
- Which children are beginning to handle frustration in a more acceptable manner than previously?
- What comments from the children indicate that they are making attempts to solve problems?
- Which of the learning activities interested the children most? the least? Which children participated more today than in the past?
- Recall something specific that each child did or said during the day.
- Were there any new terms or ideas to define? If so, how did the children respond?
- Give some specific instances in which you gave positive reinforcement to a child for appropriate behavior. Were there any instances where a child should have been reinforced but wasn't? What were the circumstances?
- A simple learning checklist, compiled by Landreth (1972:155-160), can be a valuable help to you as you teach young children.
- What have you learned about yourself that could be improved?

By sharing experiences and ideas with your staff, you will be better able to make meaningful plans to meet the needs of your particular children—not only the whole group, but individual children as well. One teacher may be more aware than the others of what is occurring in certain activities or with certain children, and the sharing of such awareness leaves everyone informed.

The evaluation period can be one of the most valuable parts of the day for the staff because of the interaction. A united and observant staff is an important asset to any school setting.

Plan for Tomorrow

This generally occurs the last few minutes of the evaluation period and is a brief overview of what will be occurring the following day. By being aware of concepts and activities for the following day, the entire staff is alerted to ideas and materials which will help each day be more successful.

This time might also be used wisely in the evaluation of certain children—for instance, how they are progressing, or if they need specific aids or activities.

16

The main focus of this time should be on the goals which the teacher hopes to accomplish in short- and long-range planning for individual children as well as for the group.

Books Available Throughout the Day

This list of books consists of reading material that either supports the daily theme or is an appropriate diversion from it. The list should include author, title, and publishing information.

WHAT THE REST OF THE BOOK IS ABOUT

The following chapters provide specific information which allows the teacher to apply practically the ideas and general information presented in this chapter. The chapters are arranged topically, beginning with the individual child's relationship to himself. However, the chapters are not related sequentially; they can be used in any order. Each chapter is self-contained for use apart from the others. But you will want to refer frequently to this chapter on the lesson plan when review of general ideas and techniques is necessary. Some reference guides are provided in each chapter when a little back-tracking is necessary.

The information is given to stimulate you to use initiative and creativity in helping preschool children discover their world, not to make you feel obligated to follow the sample lesson plans exactly as they are set up in each chapter. One of the most exciting things about teaching each preschool child is that as you discover his world, you can also rediscover your own.

THE CHILD 2

An infant is first aware of only himself—he knows when he is hungry, when he needs changing, when he hurts, when he is held and cuddled. Each day he grows in awareness, learning to relate his body and abilities to his environment. During his early years, it is most important that someone help him acquire a positive self-image, help him learn to move his body skillfully, and help him learn to use his abilities successfully—all of these for many reasons. One of the most important is that it is essential that the child feel good about the person he is. He should enjoy being himself rather than wishing to be someone else who looks more appealing, according to popular standards, or someone who has more capabilities. If a person is satisfied with himself, he accepts and appreciates his sex role, shows proper sex identification with his own and the opposite sex, feels more secure in exploring his environment, seeks independence, and is generally more sociable.

A secure child also learns more freely. The teacher plans experiences which will be successful and does so by beginning with what each child already knows, moving from general to specific ideas and from smaller to larger, more encompassing truths, as the child indicates readiness and interest. As does most everyone, each child thrives on successful experiences—they give him confidence to try again and the desire to progress continually. His readiness for learning depends on his attentiveness, motivation, and maturity. If the child doesn't have these three prerequisites, his learning will be slow and frustrating (Gagné, 1970:289).

A child increases his self-confidence by having firsthand experiences. He comes to know how things work or don't work because he tries them—not because someone tells him. He may come up with a novel way to solve a problem or use materials and should be encouraged to explore and experiment.

"When a child is confronted by a problem he cannot solve by experimenting, he draws on his experience to make sense of what he sees and hears" (Landreth, 1972:15). A child learns by doing because what he does becomes part of what he knows; each experience is internalized in the form of a mental image or action strategy (Piaget, 1962). His images or strategies are combined and rearranged as the child learns from experience.

The way a child perceives a situation has a great deal to do with how he responds. If the experience is challenging, he attempts it with enthusiasm. If it is threatening, he withdraws, or, if he attempts it and fails, he is frustrated or negative and often afraid.

As each child becomes more aware of himself in a positive manner, he becomes more aware of his environment. When he takes a walk, he is able to see the beauties of nature or smell the fragrant spring blossoms, because he uses freely two of his body's senses. Adults taking the time to explore the immediate environment with him, heeding what he is interested in, help him become more aware and appreciative of his surroundings. Often adults are too busy to watch a ladybug on a blade of grass or a worm after a rain storm, but young children are fascinated by such things. This is learning in its pure form.

As each child learns about himself, he is stimulated in the use of language. He discovers the labels for various subjects in his environment. He talks about his elbow, for example, because he knows where it is, what it is called, how it is used. He needs opportunities which allow him to hear and use language so that he can learn and use words to communicate with other people. If you have called a child by the wrong name, you have found that he is usually quick to correct you. He likes to be called by his own name—and to hear it often, especially when it is connected with good things he has done. Adults help children learn the names of other people by using them frequently. When a child says, "Hey, you," or "kid," or "teacher," the adult can say to him: "His name is _____ , and if you call him by his name, he will know you are talking to him."

Each child also learns that some words have many meanings—a person has two legs, most animals have four legs, and a table also has legs, though they differ from legs of live beings. And when the child hears about the "leg of a journey," he is puzzled because he sees no visible leg at all! For example, Morgan, age three, had struggled earnestly to put on his boots so he would be ready to go outside after a rainstorm. Proudly he said to his teacher, "Look, I'm ready!" The teacher replied, "But, Morgan, you have your boots on the wrong feet." He stood there, puzzled, looking at his feet, and then said very seriously: "But these are the only feet I have!"

Because each child's self-image, body, and abilities—and his understanding of them—are at the core of everything he does or thinks, it is most essential that those who teach him be fully and positively aware of these highly important areas of self-development. This chapter has been designed to:

- Help each child like himself by building a positive self-image and a healthy attitude toward his body, his characteristics, and his abilities.
- Give each child an opportunity to solve problems by himself and/or with others through having, using, and sharing ideas.
- Stimulate each child's curiosity about himself and his environment.
- Help each child increase his vocabulary by introducing ideas or words (such as the proper names of various parts of the body), explaining behavior, identifying sensory experiences, or giving him something exciting to talk about.
- Help each child gain physical skills through his use of large and small muscles and through experiences which will be challenging and satisfying, thereby encouraging him toward reaching his individual potential in all aspects of his growth and development.
- Lay some basic foundations for future in-depth study as each child indicates he is ready for more complex ideas and information.
- Provide information that you can use effectively in teaching each youngster.
- Stimulate both adults and the young child to learn more about him and his body.
- Provide a guide to aid you in preparing a unit or in finding ideas focusing upon the child and his self-image.
- Suggest ways parents can use materials, visual aids, and various activities in teaching the child in the home.

The following four themes, I'm Important, My Body Works for Me, My Hands and Arms are Useful, and It's My Birthday, offer many valuable ideas for helping children discover themselves.

THEME 1: I'M IMPORTANT

Preassessment

Preassessment is done in advance in order that good plans can be formulated (see p. 7). Suggested ideas are:

- Say a child's name and see how many of the children know to whom it belongs.
- Help the children determine how many of them have certain characteristics in common (eye color, hair color, height, color of clothing).
- Ask the children how many have pets. See which children have the same kind of pet.
- Ask who rides the bus, comes in the same car pool, or lives nearby.
- Have the children tell about something special they have done or a place they have been.

- Let each child tell the names of his family members.
- Find out which children have new babies at home.
- Have different children help with certain activities each day (set tables, be lunch or snack helpers).
- Using dark paper, make silhouettes of the side view of the children's heads.

Behavioral Objectives

The formation of a good self-image is an ongoing process. However, at the end of this experience each child will be able to:

- Name several children who have characteristics in common (eye color, hair color).
- Tell something fun he has done with another person and also name the person.
- Tell something about himself that he likes.
- Guess the names of children who are described by the teacher.
- Show or describe something to someone else that he has made or done.
- Help another child or teacher with a certain activity.
- Begin to display appropriate social techniques in interaction with other people.
- Begin to verbalize more with others.
- Begin to feel comfortable in expressing and trying his own ideas.

Evaluation

Evaluation occurs *after* the day's activities (see pp. 15-16). Suggested ideas are:

- Which children are the most verbal? nonverbal?
- When asked to assist another child or a teacher, how did the individual child respond?
- Which children are beginning to handle frustration in a manner more acceptable than their previous one?
- What comments did you hear from the children indicating that they are making attempts at solving problems?
- Which of the learning activities interested the children the most? the least?
- Which children participated more today than in the past?
- Recall something specific that each child did or said during the day.
- Give some specific instances where you gave positive reinforcement to a child for appropriate behavior.
- Were there any instances where a child should have been reinforced but wasn't? What were the circumstances?
- Did you get a different perspective of any of the children today? Give examples.
- Because self-image changes from time to time and situation to situation,

22

what do you plan to do to help the children (as individuals and as a group) continue to develop a good self-image? Outline specific goals and ways of helping each child.

- How is a good self-image related to the child's success in learning?
- What have you learned about yourself that could be improved?

There may be other appropriate questions. (Now you have preassessed for further teaching about the self.)

Having considered some of the general aspects of a lesson plan, the teacher can now see one that is actually used in a daily teaching situation.

Sample Lesson Plan 1

THEME: I'm Important

Preassessment

- Ask the children to name as many of the other children as they can.
- Describe a child (physical characteristics, clothing) and see if the other children can guess who it is.
- Ask each child to tell something he likes to do or eat.
- Have each child bring a picture of himself when he was a baby.
- Take a current picture of each child.

Concepts

- Everyone has a name and he likes to be called by his name.
- Even though people look different, they each have some special qualities.
- Each child looks different from the other children.

Behavioral Objectives

At the end of this experience, the child will be able to:

- Call most of the teachers and children by their correct names.
- Describe and name two children who have different characteristics.
- Select his own name tag from a group of name tags.
- Begin to release his feelings in an acceptable manner.

Learning Activities

- Have the children's baby pictures posted on a low bulletin board so that they can see them as they arrive.
- Have clearly printed name tags available and help each child to find his own (use printing with capital and small letters). Discuss the letter his name begins with and show him how it is made so that he will be able to identify his name tag at other times.

23

- In all activities, use the names of the children and encourage them to call others by name. ("Susan and Peter helped with the snack today. Thank you, Susan and Peter.")
- Supply creative materials that will provide opportunities for the children to cut, mix paint, and even make a picture of themselves if they desire.

Schedule of Activities

Review plans for the day

Check-in

Provide a few books and puzzles for the children until all arrive. Pin a name tag on each child.

Setting the learning stage

- Review preassessment.
- Give each child his current picture and have him pin it on the board by his

baby picture (and silhouette). Have the child's name printed on a piece of colored paper as it appears on his name tag and place this below his pictures so that he will begin to identify words or symbols with concepts or ideas.

- Sing songs which use children's names:
  - "Mary Wore Her Red Dress." Seeger, Ruth. *American Folk Songs for Children.* Garden City, N. Y.: Doubleday and Co., 1948.
  - "A Surprise on Mary." Renstrom, Moiselle. *Merrily We Sing.* Salt Lake City, Utah: Pioneer Music Press, 1957.

Free play

- Housekeeping area: provide dress-up clothes, dolls, homemaking toys, and several mirrors (large and small).
- Food experience: help the children prepare something for snack or lunch.
- Blocks: provide small unit blocks with rubber or wooden people to stimulate interaction. Large hollow blocks could encourage cooperation among children.
- Creative expression: include scissors, paste, paper, and catalogs which have many pictures of people. These encourage the use of small muscles and also help the child develop an awareness of people. Use easels with paint and paper. Have children mix their own paints. Encourage them to make pictures of themselves. Make parts for paper dolls from large, plain, heavy paper. Have the children use yarn, fabrics, and other materials to make their own image and put it together with small metal brads so parts are moveable.
- Science table: provide measuring cups and water, tops, magnets, and other materials that will encourage children to say, "Let me try that!"
- Book corner and books: see list of books on page 27.

Prestory activities

- Poetry: Aldis, Dorothy. *Everything and Anything.* New York: Minton, Balch & Co., 1927.

  "Grown Up," p. 17
  "A Good Thing," p. 39
  "Mouths," p. 87
  "Everybody Says," p. 89
  "Somersault," p. 95
  "Hiding," p. 5

- Game: begin an activity (similar to "Farmer in the Dell" but not as structured) in which one child helps and then chooses a friend. Then both children choose a friend and so on. The game moves rapidly and all of the children are included in a short period of time.

Story time

- Cole, William. *Frances Face-Maker.* New York: World Publishing Co., 1963.
- Kraus, Ruth. *The Growing Story.* New York: Harper, 1947.

Music

- Record: "When I was Very Young." Children's Record Guild—CRF-1031.

Snack or lunch

- Encourage the children to set the table, serve themselves (pour milk or juice), and clear their own dishes.
- Conversation should be encouraged.
- If the children helped prepare something for the snack or lunch earlier in the day, ask them how they made it or what they did to help. Compliment them on their accomplishments.

Outside activities

- Encourage the children to try new things. *Watch* them and help them have successful experiences. Give them honest praise.
- Arrange the outdoor equipment in such a manner that it stimulates the interests and activities of the children. Rearranging old equipment can be just as exciting as getting new equipment.

Check-out

- Children pick up their learning cards and depart after putting toys away.
- Suggested learning card:

(School or teacher's name) _____   _____ (Date)

Theme: I Learn about Myself

Today we talked about ourselves and learned the names of many of our friends and teachers. It is good to be called by one's own name.

It was fun to look at our baby pictures and those that show us now that we are older and larger.

We sang songs involving our names, played games with friends, and participated to activity records.

We looked at ourselves in mirrors and talked about how we look.

We can do many things to help ourselves and others. It makes us feel good when we do something well.

26

Evaluation

- Which children seem to feel the most self-confident as evidenced by their verbal and/or physical expressions and actions?
- Which children seem to need more individual help in accepting themselves?
- Which children were able to call most of the children and the teachers by their names?
- Which children could find their own name tags?

Books Available Throughout the Day

- Anglund, Joan. *A Friend is Someone Who Likes You.* New York: Harcourt, Brace & World, 1958.
- Becky. *Tall Enough Tommy.* Chicago: Children's Press, 1946.
- Berends, Polly B. *Who's That in the Mirror?* New York: Random House, 1968.
- Bright, Robert. *I Like Red.* Garden City, N.Y.: Doubleday and Co., 1955.
- Keats, Ezra Jack. *Whistle for Willie.* New York: Viking Press, 1964.
- Krauss, Ruth. *The Carrot Seed.* New York: Harper & Bros., 1945.
- Stanley, John. *It's Nice to Be Little.* Chicago: Rand McNally, 1965.
- Zolotow, Charlotte. *Someday.* New York: Lothrop, Lee and Shepard Co., 1965.

    For additional aids on this theme, see pages 157-160.

Plan for Tomorrow

THEME 2: MY BODY WORKS FOR ME

Preassessment

- Ask the children to tell you as many of the names of the parts of the body as they can. (Make it a fun game.)
- Demonstrate how you can move parts of your body and ask if they know why you can do this (joints and muscles).
- Say the names of different parts of the body and have the children point to them.
- Ask them if they know what a *sense* is or if they can name any of the five senses.
- Show pictures of people in which one or more parts of the body are missing and ask the children if they know what is wrong with the picture.
- Ask the children to demonstrate some of the things they can do. Then ask them if they can verbally describe their actions.

Behavioral Objectives

At the end of this experience, the children will be able to:

- Name the major parts of the body.
- Explain the different uses of at least five parts of the body.
- Describe the differences and similarities in the body build of two children.
- Point to at least three different bones in the body and call them by their proper names.
- Demonstrate movement of the body and explain how it occurs (joints, muscles, knuckles).
- Point to at least four different joints.
- Demonstrate and describe how the children use their bodies.

Evaluation

- Which children seemed to know the most about their bodies at the beginning of the day? Were these same children the ones who seemed to know the most about their bodies at the end of the day?

- Which children were able to verbalize what they could do with their bodies? Which ones were unable to?
- Which children were able to demonstrate use of their bodies? Which ones were unable to?
- Could most of the children name the major parts of the body?
- Could most of the children name joints in the body?
- Which one of the learning activities interested the children the most? the least?
- What comments did the children make that related to their bodies?
- If you were to use this theme again, how would you change your plan to make it more effective?

There may be other appropriate questions. (Now you have preassessed for future teaching about the body.)

Sample Lesson Plan 2

THEME: My Body Works for Me

Preassessment
- Ask the children if they know what the words *force, space, movement,* and *speed* mean.
- Ask the children to tell some things that are easy for them to do and some that are hard. Can they explain why they are easy or hard?
- Have the children verbalize their understanding of some common prepositions *(over, under, beside, behind).*

Concepts
- *Force* means how hard you have to work to do something.
- *Space* means distance or how much room is needed for a certain purpose.
- *Movement* means the action of a person or group.
- *Speed* means how fast or slow something is done.
- Words (prepositions) are used to give directions.

Note: Other explanations exist for these terms, but the definitions supplied above emphasize the theme of this particular lesson plan.

Behavioral Objectives

At the end of this experience, the children will be able to:
- Verbally define and/or physically demonstrate the terms *force, space, movement,* and *speed.*
- Participate in something that is physically difficult (pushing a heavy wagon,

hopping a distance on one foot, pounding a long nail).
- Move to the proper location when given directions containing prepositions.

Learning Activities

- The bulletin board (placed at the children's eye level) will contain pictures of activities which are easy or hard to do.
- Objects which are easy and hard to open will be used and discussed.
- Prestory and story activities will be geared to how human bodies function.
- A musical and physical activity will be provided.
- An obstacle course with verbal instructions from the teacher will help children understand prepositions.

Schedule of Activities

Review plans for the day

Check-in

Upon arrival, each child will be weighed and measured to get him thinking about his body.

Setting the learning stage
- Review preassessment.
- Sing "Head, Shoulders, Knees, and Toes."
- Have a number of items that need to be opened. For example, a sack, a gift-wrapped package, various glass containers (screw-on lid, pressure-sealed cap, paper-covered top, cork, clamp), metal cans (sealed, tab-opened, pry-top), small boxes, and any other items which will help you discuss force, space, movement, and speed with the children. Some of these items should be harder and easier to open than others, requiring different techniques and movements and varying amounts of time.

Free play
- Housekeeping area: provide dress-up clothes, dolls, and regular items.
- Blocks: use large hollow ones plus a sheet for making a tent or house.
- Creative expression: have large pieces of butcher paper. Each child lies down on a piece of paper and the teacher traces with a pencil or crayon around him. Then the child paints an image of himself. The children can then fingerpaint, mixing, using, and cleaning up the paint.
- Manipulative area: pegboards, puzzles, hinges.
- Book corner and books: see list of books on pages 34-35.

Prestory activities

- Poetry: "Hinges," by Aileen Fisher. In Jayne, M. T., and Imogene Hilyard (ed.), *Making Music Your Own.* Morristown, N. J.: Silver Burdett Co., 1966, p. 13.
- Activity: show the hinge to those who haven't already seen it. Have them show how their bodies are like hinges. Ask them how they would move if their legs, arms, hands, and fingers were straight. Have them try different activities as they keep their bodies straight.

Story time

- Green, Mary M. *Is It Hard? Is It Easy?* New York: William R. Scott.

Music

Today include music with a physical activity. You will need lots of space, so move your furniture back, move to a large room, or go outside. You could have all of your children participate in the same activity or divide them into smaller

groups with a teacher to supervise each group. Some activities you can use to help the children understand the concepts and achieve the behavioral objectives are listed here:

- Give each child a ball about ten inches in diameter. Have him roll it as slowly as he can, then at varying speeds. Ask the children how force, space, movement, and speed are involved.

- Ask the children to bounce their balls as closely to the ground as they can, as high as they can, as slowly as they can, then as fast as they can.

- Provide each child with a marked area of his own (marked with a hula-hoop, a string, or chalk). Ask him to do as many things as he can within his area. What does he do when you ask him to do something that requires him to sit, lie down? Encourage him to move his body in many different ways as he tries out these different positions.

- Have the children run, walk, skip, hop at varying speeds. Avoid competition. This activity is for individual development.

- Use music of different tempos with the above activities.

Snack or lunch

- The children will be fatigued and will need to have something cool and enjoyable.
- Encourage the children to help set the table, serve themselves, and clear their own dishes.
- Spontaneous conversation should be provided for.

Outside activities

- Make an obstacle course with the help of the children.
- Have teachers at various points telling the children some fun things to do: "This time try going over it anyway you can without using your hands." "This time try going through it without touching any of the sides." "Climb up the stairs, walk over the bridge, wiggle through the tunnel, jump off the box."
- These activities give them great physical exercise, experience in following directions, and an opportunity to practice prepositions using their own bodies as the objects.

33

Check-out

- Children get learning cards and depart after putting toys away.
- Suggested learning card:

> (School or teacher's name) _____ _____ (Date) _____
>
> Theme: My Body Works for Me
>
> Today we learned about our bodies.
> Some things are hard to do and some are easy. Our teacher showed us some ways
>   to make hard things easier to do.
> We had experiences with balls, an obstacle course, and other activities which
>   help us understand force, space, movement, speed, and positions of things.
> We learned how *prepositions* explain how we use our bodies.

Evaluation

- Which of the children could demonstrate their understanding of the terms through either physical or verbal means? Which ones could not?
- How freely did the children enter into activities they thought were too hard for them?
- What was the response of various children to Setting the Learning Stage activities? Were some children left out of the experience? Did the children offer any novel ways of opening difficult objects?
- Which of the learning activities interested the children the most? the least?
- Did any of the children use the terms introduced today?
- Were there too many activities? Were the children overstimulated?
- Which children understood and responded to the instructions at the obstacle course? Are there any who need help in understanding the prepositions used for giving directions?

Books Available Throughout the Day

- Becky. *Tall-Enough Tommy*. Chicago: Children's Press, 1946.
- Berman, Rhoda. *When You Were a Little Baby*. New York: Lothrop, Lee and Shepard, 1954.
- Crume, Marion. *Let Me See You Try*. Glendale, Calif.: Bowmar, 1970 (p. 46).
- Huntington, Harriet E. *Let's Go Outdoors*. New York: Doubleday and Co., Junior Books, 1939.
- Jaynes, Ruth M. *Watch Me Outdoors*. Glendale, Calif.: Bowmar, 1967.

- Jaynes, Ruth M. *My Tricycle and I.* Glendale, Calif.: Bowmar, 1968.
- Keats, Ezra J. *The Snowy Day.* New York: Viking Press, 1962.
- Krauss, Ruth. *The Growing Story.* New York: Harper & Bros., 1947.
- Taylor, Barbara J. *I Can Do.* Provo, Utah: Brigham Young University Press, 1972.

For additional aids on this theme, see pages 160-162.

Plan for Tomorrow

THEME 3: MY HANDS AND ARMS ARE USEFUL

Preassessment

- Toss a ball to a child and ask, "How did _____ catch the ball?"
- Put an object up high, and ask, "What helped _____ reach the object?"
- Rub one hand on top of the other hand. Have a child describe whether it is smooth or rough, warm or cold, soft or hard.
- Ask the child if he knows names for each of his fingers.
- Ask what things can be done with hands, arms, and fingers.

Behavioral Objectives

At the end of this experience, the children will be able to:

- Say that the hands and arms are parts of their bodies.
- Name and point to the different parts of their own hands and explain how the skin, muscles, and bones work together.
- Show something new that they have learned to do with their hands.

Evaluation

- Which children were able to demonstrate use of the hands and arms? Which ones were unable to?
- Could most of the children name the main parts of the hands and arms? Use examples.
- What comments did the children make during the day that related to their hands and arms?
- Did the children react positively to their bodies when they engaged in outside play or other physical activities?
- Did any of the children react negatively to their physical abilities? Why?

There may be other appropriate questions. (Now you have preassessed for further teaching about hands and arms.)

Sample Lesson Plan 3

THEME: My Hands and Arms Are Useful

Preassessment

- Start with a hand activity. Say to the children, "Open your hands in front of you. Shut your hands. Open your hands. Wiggle your fingers (thumbs, hands, and arms). What else can you do with your hands and/or arms?"
- Ask a child to name all the parts he can see on his hand.
- Ask the children to show you how they would use their hands, arms, and fingers if a cast were placed on them.
  (Use ideas from the lesson plan My Body Works for Me.)

Concepts

- Hands and arms are a part of our bodies.
- Our hands and arms help us to do many things.

- Our hands and arms have different parts.
- People have arms but some animals don't have arms, hands, and/or fingers.

Behavioral Objectives

At the end of this experience, the children will be able to:

- Demonstrate several things they can do with their hands and arms when provided various objects, materials, or ideas.
- Name and point to the different parts of the hand and arm when given a skeleton of a hand and arm.
- Name three animals that don't have arms, hands, and/or fingers.

Learning Activities

- Play simple games and fingerplays.
- Provide creative materials for sensory and manipulative experiences.
- Have a *feel* table.
- Provide pictures and a skeleton of a hand.
- Use a flashlight for viewing the bones in the hand.

Schedule of Activities

Review plans for the day

Check-in

Have pictures of animals on the bulletin board and ask the children which ones have hands and arms. What can the children do that animals without hands can't do?

Setting the learning stage

- Review preassessment.
- Show a skeleton and identify the parts of the hand and arm.
- Use a flashlight.

Free play

- Housekeeping area: provide egg beaters, dishes or dolls for washing, and utensils for pouring.
- Food experience: make sandwiches for lunch or snack.
- Creative expression: have cutting and pasting. Or have fingerpainting or hand prints. The children mix, use, and clean up paints.
- Manipulative area: use snowflakes, tinker toys, small cubes or blocks, jars and cans to open.

- Cognitive table: provide various kinds of fabrics (rough, smooth, hard, soft).
- Book corner and books: see list of books on pages 39-40.

Prestory activities

- Finger plays: Colina, Tessa (ed.). *Finger Plays and How to Use Them.* Cincinnati: Standard Publishing, 1952.

  "Ten Little Children," p. 21
  "The Busy Fingers," p. 25
  "Five Little Squirrels," p. 49
  "Five Little Sheep," p. 49
  "Finger Family," p. 57
  "Little Hands," p. 58
  "This Is the Way," p. 59

Story time

- Petersham, Maud and Miska. *Circus Baby.* New York: Macmillan Co., 1950.
- Thompson, Eleanor. *What Shall I Put in the Hole I Dig?* Racine, Wisc.: Whitman Publishing Co.

Music

- Songs: Mursell, James L., *et al. Music for Living through the Day.* Chicago: Burdett Co., 1962.

  "Put Your Finger in the Air," p. 4
  "A Work Chant," p. 24

  Wood, L. F. and L. B. Scott. *Singing Fun.* St. Louis: Webster Publishing Co., 1954.

  "Two Little Hands," p. 59
  "My Hands," p. 58
  "I Wiggle," p. 56

Snack or lunch

- If sandwiches were made during free play, they can be eaten at lunch. If they were not made, the children can help prepare some simple items, such as spreading butter or icing on crackers, fixing finger foods (apple slices, raw carrots, celery, turnips, cauliflower, orange slices), mixing instant pudding, fixing jello, or making a drink from juice or punch powder.
- The children should also set the tables, serve themselves, and clear the tables, as well as wipe up any crumbs or spilled food.

Outside activities

Provide activities which require the use of the hands and arms (sand area with buckets and shovels, rope or regular swings, punching bag, trikes and wagons, balls, climbing, picking dandelions, planting a garden).

Cheek-out

- Children put away their toys and get a learning card before departing.
- Suggested learning card:

> (School or teacher's name) _____   _____ (Date)
>
> Theme: My Hands and Arms
>
> Today we talked about our hands and arms. We learned that they are an important
>   part of our body and that different parts of our hands and arms have different
>   names.
> The teacher showed us a skeleton so we could see what the bones are like
>   in our hands and arms.
> We found out that we use our hands and arms to do many things.

Evaluation

- Which children were able to verbalize what they could do with their hands and arms? Which ones were unable to?
- Which children were able to demonstrate use of the hands and arms? Which ones were unable to?
- Which one of the learning activities interested the children the most? the least?
- How many of the children need additional experiences using small muscles?
- What were the children's comments about animals not having arms?
- How many of the children could name the major parts of the hands and arms?
- If you were to use this theme again, how would you change your plan to make it more effective?

Books Available Throughout the Day

- Gibson Myra T. *What Is Your Favorite Thing to Touch?* New York: Grossett and Dunlap, 1965.
- O'Neill, Mary. *Fingers Are Always Bringing Me News.* Garden City, N.Y.: Doubleday and Co., 1969.

- Lowrey, Laurence. *Soft as a Bunny.* New York: Holt, Rineheart & Winston, 1969.
- Shortall, Leonard. *John and His Thumbs.* New York: William Morrow and Co., 1961.
- Steiner, Charlotte. *My Bunny Feels Soft.* New York: Alfred A. Knopf.
- Tester, Sylvia. *I'm a Big Helper.* Elgin, Ill.: David C. Cook Co., 1963.
- Zion, Gene. *The Plant Sitter.* New York: Harper & Bros., 1959.
  For additional aids on this theme, see pages 162-164.

Plan for Tomorrow

THEME 4: IT'S MY BIRTHDAY

Preassessment

A few days before a birthday celebration is to take place in the school setting, casually ask the children:

- What they know about birthdays—for instance, what we do on them, why we have them.
- Who just had a birthday?
- What do they like about birthdays?
- When is their birthday?

Behavioral Objectives

At the end of the experience, the child will be able to:

- Give the date of his birthday (or the season).
- Make or do something nice for someone's birthday.
- Tell how he can share his birthday with others.

Evaluation

- How did the child feel about sharing his birthday with the other children?
- Could each child tell when his birthday is?
- Was each child eager to make or do something which would make another's birthday happy? Use examples.
- In general, was this a happy or frustrating day for the children?
- When another child in your group has a birthday, what ideas would you initiate or delete to make the day flow smoothly?
- Is it a good idea to celebrate a preschooler's birthday at school?
- How could you celebrate holidays or other special occasions?

There may be other appropriate questions. (Now you have preassessed for further teaching about the birthday.)

Sample Lesson Plan 4

THEME: It's My Birthday

Preassessment

- Ask the children what it means to have a birthday.
- Ask each child when his birthday is.
- Ask what each one likes to do on his birthday. Do the children do different things when it is their father's or mother's birthday?
- Show a picture of a pet with a party hat on his head. Ask, "Do you have a party when it is your pet's birthday? Why?"

Concepts

- Birthdays are fun days.
- Each person has one birthday each year.
- We can share our birthdays with others.

41

Behavioral Objectives

At the end of the day, the child will be able to:

- Tell when his birthday is (date or season).
- Tell something that happened today which made him happy because someone shared a birthday.

Learning Activities

- Bulletin board depicting the activities of a child's birthday.
- Specific ideas to be used during Setting the Learning Stage which focus on birthdays.
- Appropriate materials for domestic play and dramatization.
- A special food experience to be prepared and used at snack time or lunch.
- Creative activities to encourage the children to make festive creations.
- Stories, books, music, and finger plays to support the theme.
- Special attention to be given the birthday child throughout the day but especially during snack time or lunch.
- Spontaneous conversation throughout the day to be about one's own birthday and sharing someone else's birthday.

Schedule of Activities

Review plans for the day

Check-in

- As the children arrive, they will see on a low bulletin board pictures representing a young child's birthday. This should encourage verbalization at the beginning of and throughout the day.
- Having the room decorated with crepe paper, balloons, and so on may be too stimulating for the children. If you want to do something festive like decorate, involve the children so that they will feel a part of what is going on. Discourage teachers from making the setting too adult-centered.

Setting the learning stage

- Review preassessment.
- Tell the children it is a special day because it is _____'s birthday.
- Ask, "What can we do to make this a happy birthday for _____ ?"
- Make any special preparations.

Free play

- Housekeeping area: provide plastic fruits and vegetables, dishes, dolls, and

42

dress-up clothes for boys (hats, ties, jackets) and party clothes for girls (fluffy hats, high heels, full skirts, scarves).

- Food experience: make a special dessert or treat for lunch or snack time.
- Creative expression: let children make and decorate party hats (their own creations) from paper plates, newspapers, old bleach containers, tissue paper, feathers, lace. Make a collage using glitter, cotton balls, colored macaroni, and pipe cleaners.
- Manipulative area: supply a variety of small muscle toys—snowflakes, plastic blocks or shapes, small hammer and nails on fiber board.
- Book corner and books: see list of books on page 46.

Prestory activities

- Talking Time: let the birthday child tell what special things have happened to him today. Encourage other children to talk about their birthdays.
- Finger play:

Today is _____ 's birthday.
Let's make him/her a cake.
First we need to stir it.
(Use one arm in circle to waist to represent a large bowl and the other arm in stirring motion.)
Then we'll watch it bake.
(Shade eyes with hand as if looking into oven.)
We'll put frosting in the middle and all around.
(Do motion as words suggest.)
It's so soft and smooth it doesn't make a sound.
We'll write "Happy Birthday" and stick some candles on.
(Make writing motion with hand and then pretend to stick candles into top of cake.)
1 - 2 - 3 - 4 - 5 (Count number of candles to go on cake.) Now let's sing a birthday song.
(Sing traditional "Happy Birthday Song" or one listed in music references.)

- Poetry: Dwyer, Jane E. *I See a Poem.* Racine, Wis.: Whitman Publishing Co., 1968.
  "The Birthday Child," p. 16

Story time

- Buckley, Helen E. *The Little Boy and the Birthdays.* New York: Lothrop, Lee, and Shepard, 1965.

Music

- Songs: Berg, R. C., et al. *Music for Young Americans: Sharing Music.* New York: American Book Co., 1966.

  "Happy Birthday," p. 110
  "Today's My Birthday," p. 111

Snack or lunch

- Let the birthday child be a helper today. You may or may not want to use something special like party napkins or paper cups.
- If a special treat was made as a food experience earlier in the day, the birthday child could serve it to each child. If nothing special was made and the child brought a treat for his birthday, he could serve that.
- If no special treats are to be served, the birthday child could be recognized by the teacher and the children could sing "Happy Birthday" to him if this had not been done earlier in the day.
- Thank the child for sharing his birthday with the others at school: "It made

this a happy day for all of us because you shared your special day with us. Thank you."
- Encourage the children to put their utensils and/or dishes on a tray and clean up after themselves before going outside.

Outside activities

Today try something special but active. Have a record player outside with a variety of rhythms on records. Provide the children with colored paper streamers or balloons and encourage them to move as the music suggests to them. This gives the outdoors a festive atmosphere and the children have plenty of room to move.

Check-out

- Help the children pick up materials and tidy up the yard before they depart.
- Each child is given a learning card about the day's activities.
- Suggested learning card:

(School or teacher's name) _____   (Date) _____

Theme: Birthdays

We had a fun time at school today because one of the children shared his
    birthday with us.
We dressed up for a party, made a special treat for a snack (or lunch),
    heard a story, and sang a birthday song.
Outside we used paper streamers and balloons as we moved to
    different rhythms of music.
We learned that it is fun to share a birthday with others.
We can make things for them, do nice things for them, and help them be happy.
Instead of always receiving, a birthday person can share his special day
    with others, making them happy too.

Evaluation
- How did the birthday child respond to sharing his birthday with others at school?
- How did the other children respond?
- Was it difficult for some of the children to realize that it was not their birthday today?
- Which activity was most enjoyed by the children? least enjoyed?
- Did any of the children comment on today's activities? What did they say?

- Which children understood the concept of sharing their birthday with others rather than expecting others just to give to them? Use examples.
- Did the children who entered into the food experience feel they were helping prepare for a party?
- How many of the children freely joined in the outdoor music experience? Were there any problems involved with this activity?

Books Available Throughout the Day

- Brown, Myra Berry. *The Birthday Boy.* New York: Franklin Watts, 1963.
- Colver, Anne. *Nobody's Birthday.* New York: Alfred A. Knopf, 1961.
- Charlip, Remy. *Dress Up and Let's Have a Party.* New York: William R. Scott, 1956.
- Fern, Eugene. *Birthday Presents.* New York: Farrar, Straus and Giroux, 1967.
- Heilbroner, Joan. *The Happy Birthday Present.* New York: Harper and Row, 1962.
- Jaynes, Ruth. *What Is a Birthday Child?* Glendale, Calif.: Bowmar, 1967.
- Kirkpatrick, Leonard H. *How Old Are You?* New York: Abelard-Schuman, 1957.
- Sandberg, Inger, and Lasse. *Little Anna's Mother Has a Birthday.* New York: Lothrup, Lee and Shepard, 1966.

    For additional aids on this theme, see pages 164-165.

Plan for Tomorrow

ESPECIALLY FOR PARENTS

Sometimes the best teaching is done on a one-to-one basis, and parents have particularly good opportunities for involvement in such situations. If you were able to preassess each child's thinking about a certain concept and could look objectively at his ability in relation to his chronological age, you would be among the most influential teachers that children would ever encounter. Obviously you are always teachers, either directly or indirectly. You see each of your children under all kinds of circumstances and even more important, have them under your constant care during the most formative years of their life—birth to the age of six.

You and your child can build a good relationship by periodically spending uninterrupted time together. The quality of the time is more important than the quantity; if the atmosphere is relaxed and casual, the stage for learning is set. A mother and/or father is a constant model for each child, and the way he

46

or she responds to him and to different situations involving him leaves lasting impressions.

You need to be aware of the development of children at various ages so that you will not expect too much or too little of them. (Many helps in this area are available, some of which are listed in the bibliography [p. 177]). Bored and frustrated children do not enjoy learning. If given a thirst for learning at a young age, preschool children will have much more pleasant educational experiences and will look forward to the many years of school ahead.

Children often ask thought-provoking questions about things that adults take for granted or ignore. When a child asks a question to which you do not know the answer, all you need do is reply, "I really don't know. Let's see what we can find out about that." It is perfectly acceptable human behavior not to know *sometimes.*

A parent who spends much time with a child will find it fairly easy to determine his interests. You can plan experiences the child is interested in, as well as others that will increase his horizons. How can the child become interested in something if he is never introduced to it?

If the children in a particular group are of different ages, they will most likely have different degrees of ability, different interests, different experiences, and different language ability. It will therefore be challenging and stimulating for you to plan information which will be meaningful to them. Many ideas that can be utilized in a home setting are included in each sample lesson plan, and knowing how to plan for each of your children's needs should give you more confidence.

About self-concept

When a child is very young, he is totally dependent upon his parents and wants to know that they love him and are filling his needs the best they can. Not being experienced, he is unable to manipulate or deliberately set traps, and when his needs are met (fed when he's hungry, changed when he's wet), he is content.

As the child grows, he begins to expand his capabilities—he learns to roll over, then to sit up, and eventually to walk and run. As the various parts of his body begin to mature, he moves about more easily and quickly (often to his parents' inconvenience) and wants to explore new things. This is a crucial time, for the manner in which a mother and/or father responds to his new interests and capabilities helps or hinders him as he forms ideas about himself. He must be restrained at times, but at others must have opportunities to freely interact with his environment. You should set guidelines and then let the child maneuver within his boundaries. For example, when you cannot allow the child to use a particular object, you should at least give him something in return.

Each child develops his self-concept as a result of his interaction with his environment—as well as from external cues ("I must be dumb, or aggressive, or shy, or whatever, because I am always being told that"). You should use a positive approach to problems rather than a negative one ("You try and then if you need help, I'll help you"), then stand by to offer assistance *if* it is needed. If you do help the child, encourage him so that he will be able to do the task by himself at some future time. If he completes the task successfully, you can say something like this: "Sometimes you don't know if you can do a thing unless you try. *Now* you *know* you can do it."

Each child should help with various household tasks, at first those that are simple enough so he can succeed and then gradually those that are more complex so that he feels he is growing.

Honest praise is one of the greatest motivators. A child who is given insincere praise is unable to increase his own confidence or confidence in other people. For example, a child who was being praised for a painting he had done himself replied, "I know you really don't like it, so why do you say that you do?" Another child, whose father kept saying about his painting: "It's great;" "I really like that;" "Yes, it is good;" replied, "Then tell me what it is, Dad."

48

Children sometimes do things that hardly anyone really appreciates, such as smearing cold cream on themselves and on furniture or spilling water all over the floor. But before you become too irate, look at the situation from the child's point of view. Perhaps he had seen his mother smear cold cream on her face; and when he touched it and it beckoned to be smeared, he happily complied. Or, when he filled his cup for a drink, he was so fascinated by the water that he filled and filled beyond the capacity of the cup—and maybe even the basin. Water has magical qualities for a child. In either case, the wise parent will hand him a sponge or cloth and help him restore things to normal. Sensory experiences are highly important to the preschool child. He is so interested in his world that he must be allowed to explore and experiment, to have experiences in which it is all right to smear and to pour. Encouragement or discouragement of his interests will have a strong bearing on his later learning and, of course, on his image of himself.

When you ask a child to help, or give him a responsibility, he must be allowed to do it *his* way. It may take him longer and he may not do it according to an adult's high standards, but at least he has an opportunity to try his ideas. If he gets discouraged, help him in such a way that he will feel successful, not belittled.

A child who has finally learned how to dress himself may appear one morning with a wild color combination and even mismatched socks or shoes, but at least give him credit for trying! At a later time you can talk about color combinations and artistic dress—right now the child is proud of a new accomplishment and you should let him know that you are proud of it, too. When he accomplishes something, he gains courage to try again—especially if that accomplishment is acknowledged.

All of the seemingly little successful daily experiences help the child gain confidence. You are usually the only constant contact the child has for the first few years and he needs positive feedback from you that he is a good person, that he has an adequate body, that his accomplishments are noted and appreciated, and that these accomplishments are worthwhile.

Put a mirror in your child's room where he can view himself often to see how he moves, where he can see what things look like from another angle, and where he can see parts of his body he couldn't see otherwise (his face, for instance!).

You have the privilege (and responsibility) of helping your children develop good self-images. If you do not think a particular child is worth much, he will more than likely have the same negative feelings about himself. One of your biggest responsibilities is to recognize the unique worth of each child and help him to develop so that he is able to live a happy, productive life.

Both short- and long-range goals are extremely important in the development of a good self-image. Each child needs to know that he is able to do things he is interested in now, and at the same time lay the foundation for later development (he picks up his toys now to make his room more tidy—and to please you, but the picking up also helps him develop good work habits).

If you help each of your children develop a good self-image from birth, they will be happier and more productive. And those who come in contact with them as they grow older (teachers, relatives, peers, employers) will find the association much more pleasant.

Young children are quite flexible and forgivable. You should relax, enjoy being with each child, and learn from each as you watch the self-image grow.

About the body

It is important that each child know and use the names of the various parts of his body. If he is to communicate with others, he needs to know the common terms. As the child realizes that it is important to learn names, he is motivated to increase his vocabulary and his understanding.

Because of the one-to-one relationship in the home, you can plan many opportunities for each child to demonstrate what he can do with his body. Parents too often do tasks the child can handle because they don't want to be bothered with his slowness and inexperience. However, long-range goals are of utmost importance—the child must have successful experiences when he is young so that he can gain the confidence to try other tasks.

Using the ideas in this lesson plan, you can stimulate your child to learn more about his body. For instance, a mother can raise questions throughout the day: "You look out of your eyes, but what else do you know about them? Maybe we can find out something together." Often, upon learning a little about a subject, one is stimulated to want to learn more. (Joints help us move the different parts of our bodies, but what else is involved? Muscles help us to do things, but where are they located and how do we strengthen them?) A mother can use many daily situations to help her child grow. One day she reads to the child about the ear, for example, and the next day when she is dressed up for a special occasion, her child notices that she is wearing earrings and wants to try them on. He wants to know how they stay on, why she wears them, if they pinch her ears, why she screws them on when someone else's earrings are held on by a wire that passes through her ears. She and her child can talk about and feel the lobe of the ear. Most schoolteachers are never able to have these kinds of experiences with an individual child because they must take care of many children at once.

About hands and arms (small motor skills)

Sometimes hands are always where they shouldn't be ("Don't touch mother's vase." "The stove will burn you because it is hot." "Keep your hands out of

50

the food until dinner is ready." "You'll break that if you touch it."). But it is highly important that children be made aware of acceptable places for their hands to be ("Use your hands to knead the bread as hard as you can." "Hold on tightly so you won't fall out of the swing." "Carry the pitcher carefully so you won't spill." "Put the things in the box neatly so they will all fit.").

Because a young child is unskilled and inexperienced in the use of his hands, he needs easy tasks first and then increasingly more difficult ones to help him grow. He will develop his small muscle coordination as he has the opportunity. He can sort buttons (by size, color, or number of holes), tooth-picks, thread, nails, hair rollers, or paint brushes; he can put macaroni, rice, or cereal into small containers; he can screw lids on various kinds of jars; or, under supervision, he can cut fabrics and different kinds of paper.

If possible, the child should see where his father, mother, an adult friend, or relative works and observe how different people use their hands as they perform different tasks. The adult can talk to him about how different occupa-tions require hand involvement (for example, dentist, artist, mechanic, baker, assembler, sales clerk, architect, carpenter, typist).

51

You can also plan to take your child to see a jeweler the next time you go to town and have the jeweler show the child how he measures the size of fingers so he can make rings that fit. The jeweler can also show the child his magnifying lenses and other tools. If appropriate, you can even purchase a ring for your preschooler.

In addition, you can talk to your child about objects with arms (couch, chair, lathe, machines) and hands (clocks, watches).

Someone who plays the piano or another musical instrument (the parent perhaps) can show the child how important it is that the fingers are strong and are placed on the instrument correctly so that melodious sounds result. If circumstances permit, the child should be allowed to feel free to try *his* hand at some instruments (autoharp, drums, stringed instruments).

If you and your child are sports enthusiasts, you can point out to the child how athletes use their hands and arms in different events.

As you go about your daily activities, whether work or leisure, you can casually explain to your child how he is using his hands and arms.

About birthdays

What is more important to a young child than his own birthday? Listen to young children as they play: If a problem arises, they will sometimes say something like, "If you don't let me use that, then you can't come to my birthday party!"

A parent in the home can easily stimulate a child about his birthday a long time in advance, but it is usually better if the child is made aware of it only a couple of days before—he finds it so difficult to wait!

In planning a birthday party for a preschool child, you should be sure it is child-centered, providing games that young children enjoy, seeing that *every* child gets a prize (avoid competition), providing food they can easily manage (both in quantity and composition), keeping the time short, watching the time of day (in late afternoon children are usually hungry, tired, and restless), and limiting the number of children (a large group is hard to manage). If adults are also invited, other problems may result which require creative solutions.

When a young child has a party and gets lots of presents, he usually does not want to share his newly-acquired possessions before he has a chance to use them. You should encourage him to share them, but not force him. Young children are still egocentric and need to possess before they can share. (A child who brings a present to the party may not want to leave it, either.)

The child should help with the planning—for instance, be taken to the store to get party napkins, help make the refreshments, and make arrangements for games.

He should also have an opportunity to help plan and prepare for someone else's birthday. As a result, he will be able to realize how he shares another's birthday and should find it easier to share his own.

Perhaps there are some family traditions that you have associated with birthdays (a special activity, a musical birthday cake plate, special privileges), but instead of forcing them upon your child, you should give him reasons why those special things are done. For example, you might explain a particular tradition in this manner: "This birthday cake plate is used on every birthday because _____ ." "When it is your birthday, you get to _____." "You don't have to _____." Or, "The birthday person gets to decide on something special (where the family will go for dinner or a favorite activity)."

Instead of encouraging the idea that birthdays are for getting, you can help your child realize that birthdays are for sharing, that it is good to make many people happy on birthdays by making things for them, doing things for them, and thus sharing our special day with them.

To avoid a problem when new clothes of the child's choice are promised for a birthday, you can explain to your child that you will select three or four outfits but that he gets to make the final choice. This way you can select several acceptable outfits but the child can choose the one he wants.

Everyone involved should have a fun time on the child's birthday. But remember that your child will be easily stimulated and easily fatigued, so you should carefully plan his day and its activities.

OTHER PEOPLE   3

A child, being egocentric the first few years of his life, is not able to view an idea or a situation from any angle but his own. In essence, he lives within his own little world. In chapter two, the emphasis is on the importance of each child having a good self-image, for if he does he will welcome opportunities to interact with other people and will gradually learn to look at the world from several points of view.

Each child should be accepted within the family structure because he is a member of it rather than because of his contribution to it. He may be the firstborn child and a trailblazer for younger siblings. He may be a middle child or the caboose. Whatever his ordinal position, he needs to be respected for the individual he is despite the role he plays. Whether he is an only child or whether he comes from a large or small, one-parent, two-parent, or extended family, he is still a member of a family. There is much that he can learn about his own family as well as the families of other children with whom he comes in contact. He will even be interested in his teacher and her family—how can she be a wife, a mother and still a teacher? How can a mother be a sister? Extended families are sometimes confusing. For instance, it is often difficult for a child to distinguish which set of grandparents belong to his father or mother, especially if both sets have the same last name, which, though not a common occurrence, does happen occasionally. He may also be frustrated with the labels *grandmother* and *grandfather* and come up with a rather interesting means of differentiating, such as "grandma with teeth" and "grandma without teeth."

As each child grows, he broadens his experiences beyond the family and learns that in order to be accepted by others, he must have something to contribute. He is no longer accepted or tolerated just because he has birth rights. This shift is often threatening or frustrating because he doesn't know

how to cope with it, but he eventually learns that aggression causes problems while cooperation tends to dissolve them.

One of the early experiences he will have outside the family is likely to be a nursery school or group church experience. Here he must learn how to interact with other adults. Will they like him? Will they care enough to prevent him from doing anything harmful to himself or others? Will they look to his interests and needs? Will he have the same privileges and responsibilities as all the other children? Will he be comforted when he is upset or injured and guided when he is frustrated or angry? How will they respond to him?

And what about the new children he will meet? How will he get along with children his own size and age when he has been interacting only with adults or siblings who are both older and younger? Will he compete for the teacher's attention? Will this be a fun or a threatening experience? How will he begin to form relationships with the other children? This could be an overwhelming experience for him.

As each child ventures into the community, he comes in contact with many adults with different occupations. By taking time to talk to him about the services of these people, an adult can help him increase his knowledge and appreciation of his world, explaining that we would not be able to function as a community without the services of each of these people. The child who hears a spontaneous account of the gas station attendant, the grocer, the postman (and others) will gain an increased awareness of life. Often when a young child is asked, "What do you want to be when you grow up?" his answer is, "a garbage man because he drives a big truck and he crushes the trash" (this gives him a feeling of power), or "a fireman because he drives a big red fire engine with the siren on" (power again). He seldom chooses an occupation with less visible activity because he knows nothing about it. Sitting at a desk (no matter how big the executive) has little appeal for him. To an amazing degree, an adult can help the child learn about and appreciate the various community helpers.

This chapter is designed to:

- Acquaint the child with family members and their roles.
- Talk about the different physical characteristics of other people (hair, eye, or skin coloring, height, weight).
- Help children become aware of the many things they do with another person or persons.
- Foster successful interaction with others by helping the child acquire some acceptable techniques for dealing with other children and adults.
- Show children that adults and other children are friendly and that they will accept them and be their friends.
- Acquaint the child with people within his community and the different occupations they hold. Focus on a specific community helper (the police-

man, for example) to show how a plan can be formulated to help the child get to know and be friends with him.

- Assist children in distinguishing between uniforms of differing occupations.
- Provide a model to aid the adult in preparing a unit or ideas on relationships with other people.
- Suggest ways parents can use materials and visual aids to provide teaching experiences in the home.

The following four themes, We're a Family, Friends Are Fun, Many People Live in My Community, and The Policeman Helps Me, offer many ideas for teaching about people who influence the child.

THEME 1: WE'RE A FAMILY

Preassessment

- Have you heard the word *family?* What does it mean?
- Who is in a family?

- Do all families have a baby?
- Name some of the things various family members do to help each other.
- Ask what the children know about relatives, such as cousins, aunts, uncles.
- Can a mother also be a sister or a father also a brother?

Behavioral Objectives

At the end of this experience, the children will be able to:

- Discuss the names and relationship of family members.
- Tell what they can do as a family member.
- Give an indication of their understanding of extended families.
- Name some roles that are played by a few specific members and some that are shared by several.

Evaluation

- What did the child say or do to indicate his understanding or misunderstanding of family roles and members? Is their knowledge of roles accurate or inaccurate?
- Do the children use terms like aunt, uncle, or cousin? Do they understand how the relationship is derived?

Sample Lesson Plan 1

THEME: We're a Family

Preassessment

- What is a family?
- Name the members of your family.
- Ask the children if they have older and/or younger brothers and sisters.
- How many of the children have a baby in their family?
- What are some of the things a mother does? a father? children?
- Does anyone else live with your family besides your mother and/or father and siblings?
- Ask the children what they like to do with their family.

Concepts

- Some families are large and some are small.
- A family consists of one or two parents plus children.
- Brothers and sisters are called *siblings*.
- Each family member has responsibilities (jobs) and privileges (fun).
- Sometimes other people live with families.

- Families work and play together.
- Each family member looks different from the other members.

Behavioral Objectives:

At the end of this experience, the children will be able to:

- Give the names and relationship of members of their family.
- Name some extended family members by relationship (grandparents, uncles and aunts, cousins).
- Demonstrate or relate some roles of various family members.
- Tell how families can be different in composition (one parent, all boys).

Learning Activities

- Use of family pictures on the bulletin board.
- A visit from a mother and baby.
- Dramatic play with props for stimulation.
- Books and stories about family members.
- Musical activity with suggestions from the children.
- Outdoor play.

Schedule of Activities

Review plans for the day

Check-in

- Have pictures of families doing things together set up on the child's eye level.
- Encourage the children to comment about the pictures.

Setting the learning stage

After all the children arrive, call them together, and have a mother and a baby visit for the children to see and talk with. (It would be best if the mother and baby were part of the family of one of the children in the group—and even nicer if it were a child who needed some extra support or attention from the group.) Previously arrange with the mother to have her bathe the baby in front of the children. After she has dried and dressed it, ask her to feed the baby— perhaps some solid foods and some milk from a bottle. The children should be full of questions and comments as the baby tries to eat.

Free play

- Housekeeping area: this should be buzzing with excitement. Provide a

water table or tub, some old dolls for the children to wash, and any other necessary equipment.

- Food experience: let the children make cookies, bread, pudding, or something for today's snack or lunch.
- Manipulative area: provide a wood or cardboard house with appropriate wooden or rubber people. Encourage family play.
- Woodworking: include good sturdy tools and soft wood.
- Book corner and books: see list of books on pages 61-62.

Prestory activities

- Do familiar finger plays involving family members.
- Describe the role of different family members and see if the children can identify the member, or have some children demonstrate activities and have others guess who it is and what he or she is doing.

Story time

- Penn, Ruth B. *Mommies Are for Loving.* New York: G. P. Putnam's Sons, 1962.
- Buckley, Helen. *Grandfather and I.* New York: Lothrop, Lee & Shepard.

Music

Involve the children in singing and participating in the song, "This Is the Way We Wash Our Clothes." Encourage them to suggest ideas for what they might do as different family members, and incorporate these ideas into the song.

Snack or lunch

- Serve what the children prepared earlier.
- Let them help set the tables, serve themselves, and clear away their dishes.

Outside activities

- If weather permits, move some of the housekeeping equipment outside where it can be used in connection with trikes, wagons, and other equipment. Large boxes can represent rooms or even houses.
- In the sand area put trucks, cars, shovels, and buckets to encourage dramatic and creative play.

Check-out

- Before each child leaves, he puts away his toys and receives a learning card.
- Suggested learning card:

(School or teacher's name) _____   _____ (Date)

Theme: We're a Family

We had a fun time at school today talking about families.
Some families are different sizes, and each member has work to do and things
  he likes to do.
A mother and baby visited our school and we watched the baby get fed and bathed.
We had activities in which we could pretend we were fathers, mothers,
  and other family members.
As we grow older, we learn to do many things that we could not do
  when we were babies.

Evaluation

- How did the children respond to activities encouraging them to role play? Did the children change roles often or did they stay with a single role?
- Which children could give the name and relationship of members of their family?
- Which children indicated in their play or verbalization that they understand the concepts about relatives?
- Which activities stimulated the most play and conversation?
- As the children verbalized about their own family, did they give evidence that their relationships were positive?
- Were there any problems with a child who comes from a family which is different (one-parent, only child) from those of most of the other children? If so, what can you do in the future to help the child accept these differences with a positive attitude?
- How can you build upon this theme for future teaching?

Books Available Throughout the Day

- Buckley, Helen. *Grandmother and I.* New York: Lothrop, Lee and Shepard.
- Curry, Nancy. *The Littlest House.* Glendale, Calif.: Bowmar, 1968.
- Fiedler, Jean. *New Brother, New Sister.* New York: Golden Press, 1966.
- Jaynes, Ruth. *The Biggest House.* Glendale, Calif.: Bowmar, 1968.
- Lonergan, Joy. *When My Mother Was a Little Girl.* New York: Franklin Watts, 1961.
- _____ . *When My Father Was a Little Boy.* New York: Franklin Watts, 1961.
- Puner, Helen W. *Daddies—What They Do All Day.* New York: Lothrop, Lee and Shepard, 1960.

- Schlein, Miriam. *My Family*. New York: Abelard-Schuman, 1960.

  For additional aids on this theme, see pages 165-166.

Plan for Tomorrow

THEME 2: FRIENDS ARE FUN

Preassessment

- What do other people do to make you happy?
- What is a friend?
- Can a friend be other than a person (pet)?
- What do friends do?
- How do you know if someone is your friend?
- What can you do to show someone you want to be his friend?
- Can adults be friends to children? Can children be friends to adults?
- How do you feel when you have a friend? How do you feel when you don't have a friend?
- Is it good to have friends?
- Tell the children about a friend by describing what he did to help you (fireman, paper boy, musician).
- Do all friends look alike?

Behavioral Objectives

At the end of the experience, the children will be able to:

- Describe two things people do to make them happy.
- Describe what a friend is.
- Name some friends they have (people or pets).
- Name at least three things a friend does.
- Describe or demonstrate four things they can do to be friendly to someone.

Evaluation

- What did the children do to indicate they are developing appropriate techniques for successfully interacting with other people (using more language and being less physical)?
- Were the children participating in activities which required cooperation?
- Which children seem to dominate the play because of force or aggression and which ones seem to be submissive?
- Is there positive improvement in the relationships of some of the children?
- Are there some children who can be leaders *and* followers?
- Are the children changing their behavior as they come in contact with animals? Do they verbalize reasons for handling the animals gently?

- Do the children realize that adults can be their friends?

There may be other appropriate questions. (Now you have preassessed for further teaching about friends.)

Sample Lesson Plan 2

THEME: Friends Are Fun

Preassessment
- Name someone you like. Why do you like him/her?
- How do you feel when you think someone likes you?
- What can you do to show someone you want to be friends?
- Can you be friends with someone other than children?

Concepts
- Having friends makes you feel good.
- Friends like to do things with you.
- Adults and animals can be your friends.
- Being nice to someone lets him know you want to be friends.

Behavioral Objectives

At the end of this experience, the children will be able to:
- Describe two characteristics of a friend.
- Name some of his friends.
- Tell three things he can do to make someone happy.
- Explain why it is good to have friends.

Learning Activities
- Discuss how people can be friends.
- Introduce the idea that animals are friends.
- Provide props and activities which encourage cooperative play.
- Include books and stories to support the theme.

Schedule of Activities

Review plans for the day

Check-in

As the children arrive, talk to them about friends and have a few puzzles or table activities for them to use until all of the children arrive.

Setting the learning stage

- Review preassessment.
- Tell the children about a couple of friends you have and why you like them as friends.
- Introduce an animal which is a pet and discuss why we treat animals in a friendly manner. Explain what people must do for pets that the pets can't do for themselves.
- Talk about what it means to be a friend.
- Tell the children that though physical characteristics are different with different people, these people can still be our friends.

Free play

- Housekeeping area: provide props which encourage the children to cooperate with each other (two telephones, several dolls).
- Food experience: make a recipe which requires measuring and mixing. Let the children take turns.

64

- Blocks: use unit blocks of varying sizes and shapes.
- Creative expression: today make a large mural on butcher paper which is laid upon the floor or attached to the wall. Give the children plenty of raw materials and let them jointly create a masterpiece to be displayed. An easel can be set up so that two children use one side with either a large sheet of paper they share or two individual smaller sheets. They can also share colors.
- Cognitive table: use magnets and a variety of materials, some that are attracted to the magnet and some that are not. Encourage the children to predict and discuss why some are attracted and others are not.
- Book corner and books: see list of books on pages 66-67.

Prestory activities

As a diversion from today's theme, show the children some interesting pictures and let them make up a story about them. Accept their ideas and encourage all to be a part of the experience.

Story time

- Anglund, Joan W. *A Friend Is Someone Who Likes You.* New York: Harcourt, Brace, and World, 1958. (The pictures are too small to use in a group but could be enlarged, or other pictures could accompany the text.)
- Young, W. Edward. *Norman and the Nursery School.* New York: Platt & Munk, 1969.

Music

Provide musical instruments for the children to experiment with. Then with a clapping rhythm or a record, let the children keep time to the music. They could even march around the room if space permits. Have the children change instruments several times so that each child can use whatever different instruments he desires. Have the children put their instruments into a box or cupboard before they leave the room.

Snack or lunch

- Share the food which the children prepared earlier. Show honest appreciation for their efforts and set an atmosphere that will allow for spontaneous conversation.
- Help the children to become more independent by allowing them to set the tables, serve themselves, and clear away their dishes.

Outside activities

Have the children assist each other in moving equipment to new locations or in

cooperating in some venture (teeter-tottering, swinging, playing with wheel toys, playing on the slides).

Check-out

- The children put away their toys and get a learning card before departing.
- Sample learning card:

(School or teacher's name)	(Date)

Theme: Friends Are Fun

At school today we talked about friends and learned that we can be friends with children, adults, and animals.
One way to show that we want to be friends is to do something nice for someone.
There are a lot of things that we can't do alone. It makes it fun when someone helps you.
Instead of just taking something away from someone, if you tell him you would like to use it, he might let you have a turn.

Evaluation

- Did you notice any change in the behavior of any child as a result of today's theme?
- Do some children need special help in developing good techniques for interacting with others?
- Do some children rely too heavily upon adults?
- Did you hear any verbalizations from the children about the theme?
- Which children seem to develop friends easily? Which ones have difficulty making friends?
- How many of the children can describe the characteristics of friends?
- Did any children react negatively to the theme?
- Did the activities provided encourage cooperation?
- Were the children able to comprehend the idea that animals are their friends?

Books Available Throughout the Day

- Anglund, Joan W. *Love Is a Special Way of Feeling.* New York: Harcourt, Brace, and World, 1960.
- Bonsall, Crosby. *It's Mine.* New York: Harper and Row, 1964.
- Cohen, Miriam. *Best Friends.* New York: Macmillan Co., 1971.

- Curry, Nancy. *D̶ ̶ ̶ ̶ ̶pose Miss Riley Knows?* Glendale, Calif.: Bowmar, 1967.
- _____ . *My Friend Is Mrs. Jones.* Glendale, Calif.: Bowmar, 1967.
- Estes, Eleanor. *A Little Oven.* New York: Harcourt, Brace, and World, 1955.
- Jaynes, Ruth. *Friends! Friends! Friends!* Glendale, Calif.: Bowmar, 1967.
- Madian, Jon. *Two Is a Line.* New York: Platt & Munk, 1971.
- Schick, Eleanor. *Making Friends.* New York: Macmillan Co., 1969.
- Steiner, Charlotte. *Lulu's Play School.* Garden City, N.Y.: Doubleday, 1948.

For additional aids on this theme, see page 166.

Plan for Tomorrow

THEME 3: MANY PEOPLE LIVE IN MY COMMUNITY

Preassessment

- When you go shopping with an adult, what stores do you go to?
- How do you get to the stores?
- There are people in our community who help us. Do you know what kinds of jobs they do and what they are called?
- What kind of a job does your father/mother have outside the home?
- Could one person do all the jobs necessary in a community?
- Ask each child what he would like to be when he grows up.

Behavioral Objectives

At the end of the experience, the children will be able to:

- Name at least three community helpers and describe their roles.
- When given a group of pictures of community helpers, correctly identify each of them.
- Give four reasons why we need community helpers.

Evaluation

- Which of the children were interested in learning about and identifying the various community helpers?
- Would there have been a better way to present the material?
- Were too many concepts presented in one day?
- Which children made verbal comments about the helpers indicating they understood the various roles?
- Were some community helpers difficult for the children to identify?

- Which children need additional experiences with the various helpers?
- Could the children give accurate roles for the helpers?
- Could some helpers visit the school and provide an accurate experience for the children? Could you visit others at their work?
- Are the children able to easily recognize some buildings in your community?

There may be other appropriate questions. (Now you have preassessed for further teaching about different people in the community.)

Sample Lesson Plan 3

THEME: Many People Live in My Community

Preassessment

- Ask the children to identify pictures of and describe roles of community helpers. Use some helpers that are very common and others that are not.
- Ask a series of questions such as: What do you do when you have a hole in your shoe? Where do you go when you want to buy food?
- Describe a particular occupation and see how many of the children can guess what it is.
- Relate a few specific theoretical situations involving the children and ask who they would need to help them (besides their parents). You might discuss being in a burning house; having a flat tire or a toothache; being lost, sick, or hungry.

Concepts

- Different people have different kinds of jobs.
- Many people in our community do things to help us.
- These people are called by special names (by occupations).
- It takes many people to make our community run smoothly.

Behavioral Objectives

At the end of the experience, the children will be able to:

- Name and describe the roles of at least six community helpers.
- Tell about some of the jobs of people they know.
- Accurately describe the uniform (or identifying features) of at least six community helpers.
- Demonstrate the role of a specific occupation after seeing a picture of it.

Learning Activities

- Show pictures of different occupations, objects used in these occupations, or articles of clothing worn by people in different occupations.

- Show pictures of community buildings or landmarks.
- Take a field trip.
- Provide for dramatic play to reinforce the trip.

Schedule of Activities

Review plans for the day

Check-in

Have the children use table toys until all have arrived.

Setting the learning stage

- Review preassessment.
- From a sack or box, take out objects or articles of clothing that belong to various helpers (stethoscope, garbage truck, fire engine, broom, hats). See if the children can identify the person who uses them. When they can, let

69

them take the object and demonstrate the role of that person.

- Introduce some pictures of new as well as familiar helpers and discuss how these people help us.
- Show some photographs of a familiar building in your community (hospital, novelty store, bakery) that the children are sure to recognize.
- Tell the children that you are going on a trip today and let them know what you expect of them. Prepare for the excursion by arranging to travel either by bus or by licensed, insured cars. If possible, traveling on the local bus is ideal because it generally passes some of the main buildings.
- Because the trip takes a good deal of time, eliminate many of the activities usually included each day. On the trip, point out various places of interest or ask the children if they can identify buildings. During the tour, you can sing some appropriate songs, such as "The Wheels on the Bus."
- When you return, provide activities to support your trip.

Music

Because the children are probably warm and tired, play a classical record with a soft mood and let the children rest while the snack is being prepared.

Snack or lunch

The children help here as much as possible. They may be hungry and want to linger at the tables because of the stimulation of the trip.

Inside or outside free play

- Inside: blocks with wooden, plastic, or rubber people representing different helpers should be available.

  On an old sheet, a light colored fabric, a piece of plastic, or heavy paper, trace the outline of your city or surrounding area (streets, post office, houses, churches, parks, schools). Furnish small cars and other equipment (even pieces of wood) to stimulate the children to enter into dramatic play. The children should be able to crawl on the map or around the edges. Some commercial replicas of communities can be used on the tables. From this experience you can learn some of the interests and concerns of the children from the trip.
- Outside: Have boards, boxes, tricycles, and the sand area arranged so that the children will enter dramatic play. Have some appropriate props, such as badges, stop and go signs, and whistles.

Check-out

- Children put away toys and get a learning card before departing.
- Sample learning card:

Sample Lesson Plan 4

THEME: The Policeman Helps Me

Preassessment

- Ask the children if they have ever talked to a policeman or seen the inside of his car.
- Ask the children to name the things a policeman needs for his job.
- Show pictures of men and women in uniform. See if they can accurately select those who work for the police department.

Concepts

- Policemen are our friends. They help us when we're lost; they protect us; and they direct traffic.
- Policemen are helpful.
- Policemen wear uniforms.

73

- Some policemen walk; some ride motorcycles; some drive cars, steer boats, or ride horses; some work in offices.
- Some daddies are policemen.
- Policemen need different equipment for their jobs (badge, gun, club, walkie-talkie).

Behavioral Objectives

At the end of this experience, the children will be able to:

- Name three things a policeman wears.
- Tell three different things a policeman does as part of his job.
- Tell some things he does to help children.
- Name four important items used by policemen.

Learning Activities

- Pictures of policemen and their activities will be on the bulletin board as the children arrive.

- A policeman will be invited to school.
- Badges will be provided.
- Articles of clothing for dramatic play will be available.
- Books, stories, and music about policemen will be provided.
- Outside activities will stimulate the children to act as policemen.
- Conversation will be stimulated throughout the day.

Schedule of Activities

Review plans for the day

Check-in

Provide interesting pictures, books, or games for use until all of the children are present.

Setting the learning stage

- Review material or ideas used in preassessment.
- On a low bulletin board, have pictures of policemen performing various duties. Talk briefly about them.
- Invite a policeman to come and talk *with* the children. Make sure he knows: (1) what is expected of him, (2) how to interact with preschool children, and (3) how to convey friendliness. Have him talk about: (1) his job, (2) how he helps people, (3) his uniform, (4) his family, (5) police vehicles used by different policemen, (6) special equipment, and (7) anything else meaningful to the children. Have him display or demonstrate specific items (badge, handcuffs, safety on gun, car, or equipment such as lights, siren, radio).

Free play

- Housekeeping area: be sure to include a variety of dress-up clothes, hats, badges, uniforms.
- Blocks: place large hollow ones for imaginative play.
- Creative materials: it may be difficult to provide a meaningful creative experience which supports the theme of today, so select two or three activities which are enjoyable for the children and help them be creative. Making policemen hats is a possibility but when made out of paper they are seldom durable. Badges could be made from precut cardboard covered with aluminum foil with a pin attached to the back.
- Sensory table: use sawdust with various community helpers (including the policeman) made from wood, plastic, or rubber.
- Book corner and books: see list of books on pages 77-78.

Prestory activities

- Use an action story today. Suggest that you and the children join the policeman on his rounds for a day. Involve hand and body action to indicate the different things he might do (tap hands on legs to indicate walking motion; click tongue against teeth to indicate walking over stones or a bridge; rub hands together vertically to indicate going through water or shrubbery; use a pretend steering wheel and siren to indicate cruising or speeding as the situation dictates; hold up one hand for children to cross the street or to direct traffic; put one hand to ear and the other to mouth indicating you are talking on a radio; clench fists and tap knuckles together indicating climbing a tree or ladder).
- Be creative—plan your own day with the policeman. The children are sure to suggest additional ideas (things *and* actions).

Story time

- Lattin, Anne. *Peter's Policeman.* Chicago: Follett Publishing Co., 1958.

  Note: Use other favorites or select books from the list on pages 77-78.

Music

- Songs: "The Policeman," p. 64
         "I'm a Traffic Cop," p. 64

  Pitts, L. B., et al. *The Kindergarten Book.* Boston: Ginn and Co., 1959.
- Record: "Let's Be Policemen," Young People's Records #3401

Snack or lunch

- Serve the regular snack.
- Encourage the children to help themselves.
- Conversation about policemen and other community helpers could be stimulated.

Outside activities

- Large muscle activities will support the daily theme.
- Traffic signals strategically placed on routes for wagons and trikes are fun, for the children can act as traffic policemen or as operators of the signals. If ideas regarding jails or prisons are initiated, the children often get over-stimulated. If the children initiate these ideas, try to minimize them or turn the activity into constructive play.
- Tricycles could become police cars hurrying to help people in distress—but let the children introduce these ideas.

Check-out

- The children put away their toys and get a learning card before they depart.
- Suggested learning card:

(School or teacher's name)	(Date)

Theme: The Policeman Helps Me

Today we talked about policemen and learned much about their uniforms, their duties, their vehicles, some ways that they help us, and many other fun and interesting things.

Policemen use different kinds of vehicles for transportation—even horses, bikes, and boats!

A real policeman came to our school and he showed us his badge and handcuffs, and lots of things about his car—siren, red lights, radio. He was friendly.

Some policemen are even daddies!

Evaluation

- Which children knew the most about policemen? Were their comments positive or negative?
- How did the children react when the policeman came? Were any afraid? Relate examples.
- What comments of the children indicated they were learning about policemen? Were their perceptions accurate?
- Which of the learning activities interested the children the most? the least?
- Which children accurately described the policeman's uniform?
- In what ways did the children suggest that policemen help us?
- How many police vehicles could the children name and describe?
- Would you teach this theme to these same children again at a later time? What would you add or delete to make the next experience meaningful?

Books Available Throughout the Day

- Barr, Jene. *Policeman Paul.* Chicago: Albert Whitman & Co., 1952.
- Dillon, Ina K. *Policeman.* Chicago: Melmont Publishers, 1957.
- Fenton, Edward. *The Yellow Balloon.* Garden City, N.Y.: Doubleday and Co., 1967.
- Hefflefinger & Hoffman. *About Our Friendly Helpers.* Chicago: Melmont Publishers.

- Lenski, Lois. *Policeman Small.* New York: Henry Z. Walack, 1962.
- Miner, Irene. *The True Book About Policemen & Firemen.* Chicago: Children's Press, 1965.
- Puner, Helen W. *Daddies, What They Do All Day.* New York: Lothrop, Lee and Shepard, 1960.
- Williams, Barbara. *I Know a Policeman.* New York: G. P. Putnam's Sons, 1966.

For additional aids on this theme, see page 167.

Plan for Tomorrow

ESPECIALLY FOR PARENTS

Parents are the most influential teachers of all. You spend much more time with your children than professional teachers, and your actions, attitudes, and accomplishments serve as constant models for your children.

If you treat other people in a kindly manner, your children will usually do

the same. If you gossip about the neighbors, your children will usually also do the same. And on and on it goes.

In talking about people and occupations, you can introduce many new words and terms to your children. In order for them to have exciting experiences as they interact with people, they must be able to handle language skillfully to achieve effective communication.

Children need firsthand experiences with the people who influence them. Reading about a road builder, for instance, is one thing, but to actually see a man drive big equipment, control traffic, or build bridges is entirely different. For one thing, it is hard for the child to get size perspectives from a drawing or a photograph in a book.

Occupations are changing all the time and many that were vital when you were a child are no longer in existence. Other new occupations appear all the time and you should learn about some of these along with the child.

Children who have positive experiences with adults outside the home realize that other people also care about them, and as a result they acquire more self-confidence.

79

About families

Each child usually has his first experiences in the home and it is here that he should start to acquire a good self-image so that his experiences, both at home and away, will stimulate his growth. He usually knows a lot about his immediate family but only a little about his extended family. He calls someone Aunt Betty but is rather confused, for after all, ants are insects that crawl along the ground. Aunt Betty surely doesn't do that. Then there are cousins. They are confusing, too. The language ability and experiences of preschoolers are limited as compared to those of adults. You should take your children to visit various families, introduce them to relatives, and explain relationships ("This is Uncle Bob, my brother. He is a daddy, too, and has two girls named Sue and Ann."). Children should be introduced first to close family members. Then, as the child understands, you can add to the family tree ("This is my Aunt Mary, my father's sister.").

Some families in the neighborhood may consist of only one parent, and the child should be taught that some families do have different compositions.

About friends

This is a rather abstract concept, although preschoolers can comprehend wanting someone to play with. You should invite children over to your home, or take a small group of them to the local park. Even though each of your children may have trouble sharing now and then, they will come to realize that it is more fun to be with someone than to be alone.

A visit to the pet shop or to the home of someone who has a pet will help each child see how someone else responds to a pet and how it responds to him. The dog with the happy bark and the wagging tail beckons for a personal response from almost any child.

About community helpers

Parents are usually always involved with community people and community events. Rather than accomplish daily routines with a bored or matter-of-fact attitude, you ought to try something different. For instance, a mother can have her children accompany her one day and give them a running commentary (not a continual barrage of words and explanations) of what they will be doing: "We're almost out of gas, so we'll stop at a service station where we can put the gas in ourselves and you can help." "We need to take Daddy's suit to the dry cleaners so it will be ready for him to wear to work." "When we go to the grocery store, help me remember to get some bread for Dan's lunch and some ripe tomatoes for supper." "The heel came off Evan's shoe while he was playing. We'll take it to the shoe shop to be repaired." "We'll stop and get the car washed so it will be clean for our trip to Grandma's."

You can do a great deal to acquaint each child with his community. A periodic trip to the library will help him understand its functions and give him a thirst for knowledge and a love of books. You should take him to a zoo, the airport, the fire station, the dentist, a farm, and local landmarks, and help him learn to know his way around the community, especially areas nearest home.

Few children know what a druggist does or how a mechanic works. Though they may not be able to handle visits very often or for long, most workers will take time to explain simple things to children.

There are many kinds of doctors: those who take care of children, those who fix broken bones, those who test eyes, those who care for animals, and those who are teachers, to mention only a few. Young children are not able to understand so many different classifications if they do not have some personal knowledge of what kind of a doctor is being talked about.

You should provide your child with experiences which are on his level and increase his understanding about the people in his community.

About policemen

While planning this topic for young children, you must first ascertain what they already know about policemen. A particular child may actually be afraid of policemen (as a result of parental threats regarding his behavior: "If you don't eat your spinach, I'll call the policeman to come and get you" or because of something he has seen on television). Some children may have inaccurate concepts about some policemen, such as they like to hurt people or they are mean. If you expect children to have respect for law and authority, you need to help them see those who enforce the law as being helpful rather than vicious.

Young children love to role-play. In doing so, they try to look at something from a different view, imagining what it would be like. They find satisfaction in acting "big." They are so used to seeing mostly kneecaps and belt buckles on adults that most things seem overwhelming to them. Role playing gives them the chance to be big and powerful and also increase their interaction with other children who are trying to do and feel the same. By stepping into the shoes of the policeman, or any other individual, the child gains new insights.

If you have developed an appreciation and positive understanding of policemen, your children will most likely develop the same respect for the laws and rules which are imposed upon them by society. They might not like all laws and rules, but if they understand why we have them (even for games), they can then accept and respect them more readily. As he comprehends the reasons for rules and laws, each child gains confidence in his constitutional privileges as well as responsibilities and feels sure that someone will protect his rights. He moves ahead with the assurance that if he begins to step out of line, someone will be there to help him. By having broad guidelines and freedom to move within them, he gains confidence in himself and in those around him.

You can help your children build good attitudes toward others. Take the policeman, for instance. Suppose Dad tells his child that the policeman is friendly and helps those who need him. Suppose Dad also says that the laws are made to protect all people. The policeman arrests those who speed, for example, because they may cause wrecks and injure other people or themselves. But, as he drives to a late appointment, Dad tells little Johnny to watch out of the back window to see if a policeman is coming. What kind of teaching is that? How is the child going to form accurate concepts when he has conflicting signals? Is Dad saying that it is all right to do wrong if you don't get caught? In one particular instance as a mother was taking her preschooler to school, the mother's mind was miles away from what she was doing because she was just sailing down the road paying little or no attention to the speed limit. Her youngster tapped her on the shoulder and said, "Mom, how come your thing says 4-0 when the sign says 3-0?" She had no idea he was aware of numbers or of the connection between the speedometer and the speed limit, but you can bet she slowed right down and that she has been more cautious ever since.

Some adults talk favorably about other people until there is a problem. Perhaps Mom tells her children only good things about policemen so they will have good positive attitudes toward them. Then she gets a ticket for speeding, for illegal parking, or for some other infraction. How does she act in front of her children? Does she honestly admit she was in the wrong? ("I know the speed limit was 20 miles in that school zone, and I should have slowed down.") Or does she make excuses, blame someone else, or rationalize until she is convinced she was not at fault? ("I can't see why he gave me a ticket for going 30 miles in that school zone. There weren't even any children around. I'll bet he had a bad day and wanted to take his feelings out on someone.")

You should take your children into a police station (where bicycles are licensed, lost animals are reported, and other services provided which directly benefit children). This visit should be a friendly, informative one—not made as a threat ("I will send you here to be locked up if you misbehave.") Each child should be allowed to listen to the policeman in the station calling a patrolman in his car and listen to the policeman relate to him an instance in which he helped a child in some way (the parent should arrange with the policeman in advance so he knows the reason for the visit). If possible, each child should see some of the different vehicles used by policemen (squad cars, motorcycles, canine vans). The child should be encouraged to ask questions and the policeman to answer them so the child can understand. Often, such a visit (on a one-to-one basis) is more beneficial to the child than those he takes with a group of teachers and other children, for he has an individual experience which he can share with you. He can continue to make comments and ask questions related to this visit for a long time. As a result, you can know more about what your child is thinking because he expresses himself more freely to you and to the policeman when he is by himself than he would if he were with a group.

Good preschool books about policemen should be provided for each child so that he can look through them and hear the story as many times as he likes. Each time he will probably ask new questions and offer new comments.

Although most TV programs about policemen are above the concept level of most preschool children, the children may be able to see some policemen in action without excessive violence. For young children, TV programs about policemen are much inferior to firsthand visits and other material geared to the interest and the concept level of preschoolers.

If the appropriate occasion presents itself when you are walking with your child, you should stop and introduce yourself and your child to a policeman and explain to the child what specific duty the policeman is performing at the time (helping children safely across the crosswalk, directing traffic). If you wait until after you have passed the policeman to discuss him, your child may think there is something secretive about the situation.

Many opportunities exist around your home, neighborhood, or playground in which you can encourage your children to act out the role of a policeman. Help them set up stop-and-go signals, route traffic in one direction for less congestion, or help someone locate a lost article. Children need the experience of being, as much as possible, in a policeman's shoes.

Most important in all of your teaching on the policeman, however, are the positive attitudes you possess and the examples you set for your children.

PLANTS, ANIMALS, AND WATER

4

The world is brimful of fascinating information and events, and the young child waits anxiously to be introduced to it by an adult who is also eager to discover. If you are such an adult, you seek constantly to expand your repertoire of knowledge and experience: for instance, to inform yourself about the caloric and nutrient contents of the food you eat or to update your knowledge of current discoveries about a disease or a new material used in the building industry. You realize your need to be informed, though you may know a good deal about many things. By comparison, however, the young child is without knowledge because of his limited language and personal experiences, and *everything* is new and exciting to him. He looks to you for guidance and encouragement as he gets to know his world. There is so much he does not understand, and for a while he is completely perplexed by the fact that when he squeezes a real puppy, it hurts him, although he can even toss a stuffed one up into the air without bad results.

Being guided in his discovery of the world is exciting for the child and for his teacher. One child, after listening to music through earphones for the first time, could hardly wait to tell his mother, "We heard music through earmuffs!" Because he is egocentric, the child sees and thinks in terms of his own experience. If he doesn't have many experiences, he is almost empty; thus, he needs to ride the truck, pour the juice, and plant the garden himself. Having other people tell him about them is almost useless. We need to remember that "environment has a profound effect upon human development" (Beadle, 1971).

A child must be exposed to an experience or subject many times in order to clarify it fully in his mind. Just because he has used a magnet once doesn't mean that he won't need that experience again. In fact, he will want to use it again and again, perhaps in different ways. One child, dragging a magnet over a plastic covered sheet of iron filings, was so delighted to see the result that he exclaimed: "Look, they're running after me!" What would he discover if he tried dragging the magnet through bits of paper or through water?

You should attempt to introduce and support ideas as the child shows interest in them, at the same time planning activities which will broaden his interests. One must plan wisely so as not to bombard the child with too much or not enough time to internalize the information. "Part of a teacher's task, then, is to *match* what a child *can* do to what he *could* do in learning about his world and his relationship to it" (Landreth, 1972).

Many adults are in such a hurry and under such pressure that they overlook or brush aside opportunities to take a small child on a leisure walk and thus miss what they can learn together as well as what they can learn from each other. The child stops to pick up a small feather lost by a flying bird, to watch a butterfly hovering over a delicate flower, or to laugh at a mother cat romping with her kittens in the warm sun. Some children are so overcome with the beauty of their world that they can't wait to share it—such as the preschooler who picked all the neighbor's tulips (bulbs and all) and lovingly presented them to his mother.

The value of the experience is in having it *with* and not *for* the children. Someone could spend years explaining a combustion engine to an uninformed person, but unless that person has personal contact with the engine, his concepts remain vague—and perhaps inaccurate. Children learn best by *doing.* And so do adults.

When I have assigned students to plan and execute a scientific experience *with* young children, the agony upon the students' faces is vivid. But once they have had such an experience, they can hardly wait to try another. Many have said something like "You know, I really didn't understand gravity until I had that experience with the children. Science is really fun and I am beginning to understand some of it for the first time."

One should introduce and define appropriate words for the child, giving him opportunities to try them out. Telling him that *squeeze* means to tighten his hand on or around something is not as immediate or as valuable learning as letting him actually squeeze an orange, for he gets a better understanding—he learns that not only does he tighten his hand but juice comes out as a result.

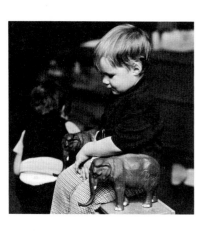

This chapter is designed to:

- Acquaint children with different kinds of animals (but focuses only on farm animals for the sake of convenience).
- Stimulate children to think and learn more about animals—where they live, what they eat, what animal parents and offspring are called, how they are classified (domestic, wild), and how they help man.
- Introduce new words.

- Give children first-hand experiences with animals.
- Acquaint children with different kinds of plants and what they need for growth.
- Discuss the edible parts of plants and the growth cycle of plants.
- Give children a firsthand experience in planting.
- Help them become acquainted with new and different foods through seeing, tasting, and discussing a variety of fruits and vegetables.
- Familiarize children with the different forms of water.
- Encourage children to think about and use water in their play.
- Demonstrate how water changes the consistency of things.
- Encourage children and adults to relate water to the environment (lakes, streams, rivers, oceans, weather, and seasons), to growth (human, animal, and plant), to appropriate wearing apparel.
- Teach new words related to water (evaporation, buoyancy, liquid, solid, absorption, repellent, dissolve).
- Provide models for adults to use as a guide in planning activities using animals, plants, or water.
- Suggest ways parents can use these materials and experiences in teaching the child in the home.

Almost any theme can be used under the general topic of nature. Three themes in particular and their sample lesson plans are very appropriate: Farm Animals Interest Me, Plants Provide Things for Me, and I Love Water.

THEME 1: FARM ANIMALS INTEREST ME

Preassessment

- Ask the children to name as many animals as they can.
- Show the children pictures of animals and see how many they can identify. Then have them put the pictures into categories (farm, zoo, pets).
- Play a record or tape of animal sounds and see if the children can identify them correctly.

Behavioral Objectives

At the end of the experience, the children will be able to:

- Identify and name three new farm animals.
- State the terms used for the male, female, and baby of at least six different animals.
- When shown pictures of various animals, tell where they live and what they eat.
- Tell the usefulness to man and the names of four different animals.
- Describe the coat of four different kinds of animals (fur, hair, feathers).

- When given the name of an animal, make the appropriate sound.
- Describe the kind of pet they would like and give reasons why.

Evaluation

- Give examples of specific children which indicate they have a clear understanding of the concepts.
- Which children could correctly identify the names (both parents and baby), usefulness, and sounds of the animals?
- Did the children know more about wild animals than domestic ones?
- How many of the children could relate firsthand experiences with animals (trip to farm or zoo, own pets)?
- Do some children need additional opportunities to build good concepts about animals?
- Are there nearby places where you could take the children to visit animals?
- What animals in your community could be brought to school?

There may be other appropriate questions. (Now you have preassessed for further teaching about farm animals.)

Sample Lesson Plan 1

THEME: Farm Animals Interest Me

Preassessment

- How many children have pets at home?
- How many of the children have been to a farm?
- Would the children like to visit a nearby farm?
- How many farm animals can the children name?
- How do animals help man?

Concepts

- Some animals live on a farm.
- Animals have different names.
- Farm animals help the farmer in many different ways.
- Farm animals live in different kinds of shelters.

89

- Each kind of farm animal looks different from the others and eats different kinds of food.

Behavioral Objectives

At the end of this experience, the children will be able to:

- Identify and name three new farm animals from pictures (parents and offspring).
- Name four more farm animals, explaining what they eat, where they live (shelter), and how they help the farmer.
- Make the sounds of at least six animals that live on the farm.

Learning Activities

- Record or tape of animal sounds and pictures of parents and babies.
- Incubator and eggs.
- Food experience.
- Stories and music.

Schedule of Activities

Review plans for the day

Check-in

As the children arrive, have wooden, plastic, or rubber animals near the door. Ask each child to identify them and make some of their sounds.

Setting the learning stage

- Review the preassessment.
- Play a record or tape of animal sounds. Have pictures available and let a child select the picture that goes with the sound.
- Bring in an incubator and some eggs that will hatch in a day or two. Explain to the children how a hen sits on the eggs to keep them warm and how you will keep them warm at school until they hatch. Also explain how you will need to take care of the chicks after they hatch.
- Talk about other farm animals.

Free play

- Housekeeping area: include some of the usual props, but do not emphasize.
- Food experience: help a few children boil and stuff eggs for snack or lunch.
- Blocks: have pictures near the blocks that suggest a farm. Add some farm animals and farm equipment to small unit blocks.

- Creative expression: use salt-flour clay or earth clay for making animals. Feathers are also fun to paste—but not necessarily into the form of a chicken or a duck.
- Manipulative area: farm or animal puzzles.
- Cognitive table: have pictures or object representations of animals and products. See which children can correctly match them.
- Book corner and books: see list of books on page 93.

Prestory Activities

- Songs:

    "A Getting Up Song," p. 114. Pitts, L. B., et al. *The Kindergarten Book.* New York: Ginn and Co., 1949.
    "Bought Me A Cat," p. 104. Seeger, Ruth. *American Folk Songs for Children.*
    "Had a Little Rooster," p. 36. Wilson, R. *Growing with Music.* Englewood Cliffs, N.J.: Prentice-Hall. Book K or L.
    (Use one song and add visual aids.)

Story time

- Petersham, Maud, and Miska. *The Box with Red Wheels.* New York: Macmillan Co., 1949.
- Berg, Jean. *Baby Susan's Chickens.* New York: Wonder Books, 1951.

Music

With the use of the piano, a record, a drum, or hand clapping, encourage the children to imitate the animals—duck waddling, pony galloping, bird flying, fish swimming.

Snack or Lunch

- Serve milk with the eggs that were prepared earlier. Raw vegetables could also be served.
- Set the atmosphere for spontaneous conversation and encourage independence in the children by allowing them to serve themselves and clear their dishes.

Outside activities

- If weather permits, plant a garden or encourage other large muscle development.
- Stick horses and cowboy hats are also fun.

Check-out

- The children return their toys and equipment to their proper places and get a learning card before departing.
- Suggested learning card:

(School or teacher's name) _____   _____ (Date)

Theme: Farm Animals Interest Me

We had a fun day at school today. We are learning about farm animals.
We saw pictures, sang songs, and heard stories about what farm animals
    are called, what sounds they make, what they eat, where they live,
    and how they help us.
Our teacher brought in an incubator and some eggs which will hatch
    in a few days.
For a snack we had dairy products and vegetables that were grown
    by a farmer.

Evaluation

- What are some of the new animals the children learned about today?
- Which children freely asked and answered questions about farms?
- Which animals could the children most easily identify by name (both parents and offspring)?
- Did the children come up with some creative movements when the different animals were suggested?
- How many of the children have visited a farm or seen some of these animals?

Books Available Throughout the Day

- Andrews, Martin. *Farm Animals.* New York: Platt & Munk, 1968.
- Anderson, C. W. *Pony for Three.* New York: Macmillan Co., 1961.
- Cook, Bernardine. *Looking for Susie.* New York: Young Scott Books.
- David, Daphne. *The Baby Animal Book.* New York: Golden Press, 1964.
- Darby, Gene. *What Is a - - - - - - - -?* Chicago: Benefic Press, 1963. (This is a series including cow, chicken, and other animals.)
- Hall, Bill. *Whatever Happens to Baby Horses?* New York: Golden Press, 1965.

  For additional aids on this theme, see pages 167-168.

Plan for Tomorrow

THEME 2: PLANTS PROVIDE THINGS FOR ME

Preassessment

- Ask the children to describe a particular plant and explain what it needs for growth.
- Ask them what parts of plants we eat.
- Have them name as many plants as they can.
- Ask them how they know when edible parts of plants are ready to eat.
- Ask them to name plants that are not edible.
- Ask them if they know how to distinguish a vegetable from a fruit.
- Now here is one for *teachers.* Which seeds germinate the most rapidly and thus provide the best growing experience for young impatient children?

Behavioral Objectives

At the end of the experience, the child will be able to:

- Describe three parts of a plant (stem, roots, leaves, blossom).
- Tell the three things a plant needs for growth.

93

- Name two edible plants which are composed of stalks, roots, blossoms, and leaves.
- Name three things we eat which grow on trees.
- Explain something about the cycle of growth (the growth of seed to sprout to stem to blossom to the mature product).

Evaluation

- Which children were the most interested in the topic today?
- Which activities involved the children for longer periods of time?
- What were some of the children's questions and comments?
- Which children knew the most about plants?
- Which children could name the parts of the plant and tell what the seeds needed in order to grow into edible products?
- How did the children who knew that some fruit grows on trees explain the growth cycle?
- In answer to the question, "Where do we get fruit and vegetables?" which children replied, "At the store?"

- Which children have or have had gardens at home?

There may be other appropriate questions. (Now you have preassessed for further teaching about plants.)

Sample Lesson Plan 2

THEME: Plants Provide Things for Me

Preassessment
- Ask which children have planted seeds.
- Ask what a plant needs for growth.
- Show the pictures or say the names of unusual vegetables and see which ones the children know.
- Ask the children to name the plant parts we eat.

Concepts
- We get food from plants.
- Plants need for growth the same things we need (air, sun, and water).
- We eat different parts of plants.
- Some plants are just for beauty.

Behavioral Objectives

At the end of this experience, the children will be able to:
- Plant seeds properly and name three things needed for growth.
- Name different edible parts of the plant and give two examples of each.
- Identify from the product or facsimile three foods which were previously unfamiliar to them.

Learning Activities
- Discussing edible parts of the plant, using produce or facsimile.
- Letting the children pretend they are seeds.
- Planting a terrarium or a garden in individual containers.
- Preparing and eating food.
- Using fruits or vegetables for a creative experience.
- Discussing a variety of fruits and vegetables.
- Hearing a story and acting in response to a record.

Schedule of Activities

Review plans for the day

95

Check-in

Ask the children to look around the room or the play yard to see if they can find something that is growing.

Setting the learning stage

- Review the preassessment.
- Ask the children to tell you the growing things they saw.
- Show produce or facsimiles grown on different parts of the plant (celery and broccoli as a stalk, carrots and radishes as a root, watermelon or squash from a vine, apples and oranges from a tree).
- Talk about and show some seeds. Have the children pretend they are little seeds. Ask them what they need for growth. As they (or you) suggest, have them move their bodies ("As the rain comes down, you stretch and grow."). Continue with the activity until they are full-grown plants.
- Explain to the children that they will be planting seeds today and tell them also some of the other fun activities that are planned.

Free play

- Housekeeping area: place plastic fruits and vegetables, empty food cartons, and other similar items in the area.
- Food experience: let the children help prepare raw vegetables for a snack. (Peas, carrots, celery, radishes, cauliflower, and turnips make an interesting treat in color and texture.)
- Blocks: arrange a variety of blocks for the children to play with, but do not emphasize this area today.
- Creative expression: use vegetable or fruit painting (potato chunks, radish roses, carrot chunks, lemon slices with thick paint made by the children. (The teacher can put the paint into *some* of the cups in a muffin pan and make it easy for little fingers and printing. The children dip the fruit or vegetable pieces into the paint and make a print on paper.) Have a variety of fruits and vegetables drawn in a simple manner on colored construction paper. Let the children cut (those who can) and paste them on white paper.
- Manipulative area: provide dirt, paper cups, and seeds. Let the children plant seeds in a cup with their name on it. Plant some extras. Have a large glass terrarium half filled with dirt. Let the children plant large seeds (beans or peas) in the dirt next to the glass. This will create interest for weeks.
- Book corner and books: see list of books on pages 98-99.

Prestory activities

Instead of using the cognitive table today, use the material for prestory activity that can be placed on the table. For example, have a variety of fruits and vegetables on a tray and discuss the size, color, name, manner of growth, and preparation for eating of each. Have both common and new ones. As suggested by the children, cut, taste, examine, and discuss some of the foods.

Story time

- Krauss, Ruth. *The Carrot Seed.* New York: Harper, 1945.

Music

Obtain "The Carrot Seed" record and let the children act in response to it. Source: Children's Record Guide #1003.

Snack or lunch

- Use the raw vegetables prepared during free play and prestory activity.
- Encourage the children to taste a variety of vegetables.
- Encourage them to be independent by having them serve themselves and remove their dishes.

Outside activities

- If the weather permits, and if you have the space, prepare and plant a garden. Have sturdy tools of good size for the children to use. Help them carefully water the garden so that the seeds remain in the soil.
- Take a walk around the play yard and look at the different plants (leaves, flowers, trees, and roots).

Check-out

- The children return their toys and equipment to their proper places and get a learning card before departing.
- Suggested learning card:

(School or teacher's name) _____   _____ (Date)

Theme: Plants Provide Things for Me

We were interested in growing things today. We pretended we were seeds, planted seeds, talked about the different parts of plants that we can eat, and learned the names of new foods.
At snack time we ate raw vegetables we had prepared.
They were different colors and had different tastes.
We looked around our room and yard to see many growing things.

Evaluation

- Which children participated in being seeds? If some children hesitated, analyze why they did.
- Which children participated in the planting of seeds?
- Of the activities provided, which seemed the best learning experience for the children?
- Which children named the edible parts of plants and gave examples? Do the children need further experience here?
- What items of produce did the children know the least about at the beginning of the day? Which ones did the children learn to identify?

Books Available Throughout the Day

- Darby, Gene. *What Is a Plant?* Chicago: Benefic Press, 1963.
- Krauss, Ruth. *The Carrot Seed.* New York: Harper, 1945.
- Selsam, Millicent S. *The Plants We Eat.* New York: William Morrow and Co., 1965.

- _____. *Seeds and More Seeds*. New York: Harper, 1959.
- _____. *Play with Seeds*. New York: William Morrow and Co., 1957.
- Webber, Irma. *Up Above and Down Below*. New York: Scott, 1943.
- _____. *Bits That Grow Big*. New York: Scott, 1949.
- Zion, Gene. *The Plant Sitter*. New York: Harper, 1959.
- _____. *Really Spring*. New York: Harper, 1956.

For additional aids on this theme, see page 168.

Plan for Tomorrow

THEME 3: I LOVE WATER

Preassessment
- Ask the children what they can do with water.
- Ask the children what they would do if there were no water at school. Show them dry powder paint and ask them how they would make a picture if the water were turned off at school.
- Show the children the freezing coils in a refrigerator and freezer and explain why frost collects on some of them. Collect some of the frost and have the children watch it melt.
- Ask the children how the water gets into the taps.
- Show the children two plants—one that has been watered and one that hasn't. Have them point out the differences in the plants. Do they know what plants need in order to be healthy?
- Ask the children how they used water before they came to school today.

Behavioral Objectives
At the end of the unit, the children will be able to:
- Show or tell how water changes the consistency of at least two different materials.
- When given different examples of objects that need to be cleaned up, correctly indicate the ones which need water (flour spilled on a rug, moisture on vinyl flooring, flour or sand on vinyl, fingerpaint on formica table, dust on furniture).
- Explain at least three ways they used water today.
- Name some games or sports that are played with the use of water.
- When given different pictures, indicate the form of water in that picture (snow, rain).
- Explain at least two ways water is used during two different seasons.
- Describe the clothing worn for water activities (swimming, walking in the rain, painting with water paints).

- Define or show the meaning of at least one new word that has been introduced in this lesson.
- Name as many uses of water as possible.
- Explain two ways water is needed in food preparation.

Evaluation

- Were plans and experiences involving water developed which will allow for the children to increase their knowledge?
- Which of the children knew the most about water? Were they also the ones who knew the most about it before this presentation? after?
- What comments of the children indicate they were learning about water? Did you hear any inaccurate information? If so, how did you handle it?
- Which of the learning activities interested the children the most? the least?
- Which children used and accurately described some of the new words introduced today?
- What were some of the uses the children suggested for water? Were any of them new or novel?

- Which children could tell or demonstrate how water changes the consistency of things?
- How did the children use water during clean-up? What were their comments?
- Which children could name the different forms of water?
- Could the children accurately describe wearing apparel used for various water activities?
- Were the children involved in the food experiences?
- Were too many activities provided? Were enough provided?
- Would you teach this theme to these same children at a later time? What would you add or delete to make the experience a more valuable one for the children?
- Are these children ready for more advanced concepts about water—are they ready to integrate concepts about water into other aspects of their daily living?
- Were the children really interested in learning about water?
- Were the concepts on the developmental level of the children? Give examples.
- Which children participated most freely in the water activities? Which children withdrew from the water activities? Why?

There may be other appropriate questions. (Now you have preassessed for further teaching about water and integrating it into the children's daily lives.)

Sample Lesson Plan 3

THEME: I Love Water

Preassessment

- Ask the children to name as many uses of water as they can, including ways they used it before they came to school today.
- Ask them where water comes from.
- Ask them what they would do if there were no water.
- Ask the children what sports require the use of water.

Concepts

- Water changes things.
- Water has several different forms (liquid, solid, gas).
- Water makes things clean.
- Water changes the consistency of things.
- Water is stored in lakes, dams, and tanks.
- Water helps things grow.

Behavioral Objectives

At the end of the unit, the children will be able to:

- Demonstrate or tell three ways they have used water today.
- Name the three forms of water.
- Define at least one new word they learned related to water.

Learning Activities

- Encourage the children to look at and verbalize about pictures containing water.
- Talk about the nature of water in the different seasons.
- Encourage dramatic play, using water and housekeeping equipment.
- Stimulate the children to participate in food experiences involving water.
- Have the children prepare creative materials using water.
- Provide a science area for exploration.
- Include books about water and its uses.
- Use water in clean-up activities.
- Have prestory activities about water; include a scientific experiment.
- Have the children relate story and music experiences to water.
- Include the use of water in snack or lunch items.
- If weather permits, plan for several outside activities.

Schedule of Activities

Review plans for the day

Check-in

All of the children do not arrive at precisely the same time; thus a few books, puzzles, or manipulative toys are provided until all children are present.

Setting the learning stage

- Review preassessment.
- Show a variety of pictures that have one thing in common—water (river, pool, hose). Discuss this similarity.
- Show two bowls—one with ice, one with water. Discuss how ice is made, how it melts, and how it can be refrozen. Explain forms of water, using new words (such as *liquid, solid, gas).*
- Tell the children some of the activities planned for the day.

Free play

- Housekeeping area: use cups, funnels, containers for pouring and measuring

102

water. Provide small tubs and scrubbing boards with doll clothes to be washed and hung on drying racks. Use words *absorb, saturate,* and *evaporate.* Demonstrate meanings. Discuss how water helps with cleaning and also how we take care of excess water.

- Food experience: with the supervision of a teacher, the children cook spaghetti or macaroni, using a package mix for sauce. (See how the consistency changes with the addition of water and heat.)
- Creative expression: in a water table, provide jars, water in a container, brushes, and dry powder paint for children to mix easel paint. Use easel. Blow bubbles using straws, water, and detergent (could be colored).
- Science or sensory table: have a variety of substances (sugar, salt, flour, sand) and a container of water. Encourage the children to see which ones dissolve in water. Use the word *dissolve* and demonstrate its meaning.
- Book corner and books: see list of books on pages 105-106.

Prestory activities

- Finger plays: Colina, Tessa (Ed.). *Finger Plays and How to Use Them.* Cincinnati: Standard Pub., 1952.
  "Swimming," p. 13
  "A Rain Story," p. 15
  "Umbrellas," p. 17
- Science experience: gather the children around the table, making sure that all of them can see. Have the following items ready: a small hot plate, an extension cord (if needed), a pan of water, a glass Pyrex bowl, and some ice cubes. Boil the water. Place ice in the bowl and hold it over the pan. As the water boils, drops of water form on the outside of the bowl and drop into the pan. Talk to the children about condensation, making sure that you deal with ideas they can easily understand.

Story time

- Tresselt, Alvin. *Raindrops Splash.* New York: Lothrop, Lee and Shepard, 1946.
- Kessler, Ethel, and Leonard. *Plink, Plink Goes the Water in My Sink.* Garden City, N. Y.: Doubleday and Co., 1954.

Music

- Record: "A Light Rain," side two, #B-561. Glendale, Calif.: Bowmar.

Snack or lunch

- Eat the food prepared earlier. Talk about who helped make the food and how they did it.

- Casual conversation at lunch or snack time adds enjoyment to the experience.
- Have the children serve themselves and clean up their dishes and utensils after they finish eating.

Outside activities

- If weather permits, provide a variety of fabrics for the children to dip into a tub of water and stimulate them to talk about what the water does to the fabrics. Introduce words and meanings that apply to this experience (*absorb* and *repel*, for example).
- Provide brushes and buckets filled with water. Encourage the children to paint various surfaces (metal, painted wood, cement, glass). Water gives the surface a different appearance.
- If water play is not appropriate, encourage the children to engage in activities which require the use of large muscles (pretend to be a fireman). Use a large boat (with holes drilled in the bottom for drainage) to stimulate

conversation about trips to many places—fishing at the lake, crossing the ocean, whaling.

Check-out

- Children put away their toys and get a learning card as they depart.
- Sample learning card:

(School or teacher's name) _____   _____ (Date)

Theme: I Love Water

At school today we talked about water.
We learned that water has different forms (solid, liquid, and gas).
We used water to change the consistency of paint, food, and other substances.
We used water in different ways—to prepare food, to wash doll clothes,
    to prepare creative materials, to water plants, and to clean up.
We had a story and musical activities related to water.
We had a science experience and even heard some new words: *evaporate,*
    absorb, and *dissolve.*

Evaluation

- Which of the children could explain or demonstrate different ways to use water?
- Did the children understand the three forms of water? Use examples.
- Which terms seemed the easiest for the children to understand? the most difficult?
- Which of the activities held the interest of the children for the longest period of time?
- Do some children need more experience with the ideas presented today?

Books Available Throughout the Day

- Andrews, Martin. *Water Life.* New York: Platt & Munk, 1968.
- Foster, Joanna. *Pete's Puddle.* New York: Harcourt, Brace and World, 1950.
- Freeman, Don. *Come Again, Pelican.* New York: Viking Press, 1961.
- Garelick, May. *Where Does the Butterfly Go When It Rains?* New York: Young Scott Books, 1961.
- Greene, Carla. *I Want to Be a Fisherman.* Chicago: Children's Press.
- Shulevitz, Uri. *Rain Rain Rivers.* New York: Farrar, Straus, and Giroux, 1969.

- Yashima, Taro. *Umbrella*. New York: Viking Press, 1961.

For additional aids on this theme, see pages 168-171.

Plan for Tomorrow

ESPECIALLY FOR PARENTS

Parents are the lucky ones when it comes to having exciting experiences with young children, for you have many more opportunities than schoolteachers to help children discover the world. Most teachers have to plan for these experiences, whereas you are able to capitalize on teachable moments. If a mother is with her child when a thunderstorm occurs, she has the perfect opportunity to talk about rain, lightning, thunder, and storms. Or perhaps the child discovers a dog with a limp, some berries on a shrub, or the morning dew on a flower. How fortunate are you and your child when you share these experiences.

Children identify with their parents, using them as constant models. When you appreciate the wonders and beauties of nature, you pass your feelings and attitudes on to your child. He then becomes curious about his world rather than believing it to be cold and cruel, and being afraid of it.

You also convey your opinions and biases to your child. If you help him look at things in a variety of different ways, seek several solutions to a problem, and make logical choices, you are very wise, for in doing so you give your child far more than information. You give him the ability and desire to seek creative solutions—one of the most important keys to productive living.

About farm animals

Some children live in areas where farm animals are an important part of family life and they see and take care of them daily. They often know more about them than do many adults. However, even these children need adults to take the time to convey to them accurate information, clarify misconceptions, and show interest.

Some children have never seen live farm animals. They live in areas where animals are not allowed or, because of transportation problems, lack of adult interest, or funds, they have been denied the opportunity of seeing farm animals in their natural habitat. If at all possible, the child should see live animals. If this is not possible, good pictures, books, or replicas giving ideas about sizes, habits, uses, and so on are helpful. Local libraries often have short films with viewing facilities. Perhaps a nearby zoo has a section of domestic animals that you can visit with your child. Too many youngsters are firmly convinced that we get milk from the store and that it comes in cartons—they have had no experience with cows, milking, and the processing of milk.

106

You should check closely around the community to see where children can see live animals. Your child's understanding will be surprising once he has beheld the subject with his own eyes.

About plants

One doesn't have to go far to have contact with growing things. They grow in the yard—no matter how small or how elaborate. Even families living in an apartment can have plants. Opportunities for landscaping are all around. (If space is really limited, put a sweet potato supported by tooth picks into the top of a jar or cut a carrot one-half inch down from the top and place it in a small saucer containing water. Watch them grow.) You may not have the space or the desire for a garden, but you can help your child plant a few seeds in some kind of a container. Plants which blossom are especially exciting for children to care for.

If you are fortunate enough to have outdoor space, even if it isn't a large garden plot, your child can have a small area all his own. Take him to the seed store and let him select packets of seeds by looking at the pictures. You can help him care daily for his garden. If some of the seeds mature for harvest, your preschooler will be overjoyed. Many a problem eater has been cured because he helped grow or prepare the food he formerly disliked.

Children should be cautioned about eating leaves and berries from trees and shrubs without checking first to see if they are edible. Many children have been poisoned by tempting-looking plants.

Depending on where you live, you might find an orchard, a vineyard, or a commercial garden nearby to visit with your child. If you are fortunate enough to live near a cannery, a greenhouse, a seed or landscape nursery, or another such commercial business, visit that with your child and become informed together.

Just opening his eyes and giving good thought to the many possibilities will help the parent realize the numerous ways his child can be helped to learn about growing things.

About water

Parents don't have to look long for an occasion in which they can introduce their children to water—they're in it all the time! We have to wash our hands and faces, take baths, quench our thirst, brush our teeth, wash our food, and once in a while just play in the water! Sometimes keeping children out of water is a major problem! But you can convey a positive attitude toward water, and rather than scolding or punishing your youngster when he splashes, spills, or soaks, make sure he knows what the limits are. ("Yes, you can sail your boat in the tub." "If you want to play in water, you need to do it here where it can be easily wiped up." Or "We won't be using water today because we are doing something else.") Prohibiting them from ever playing in water just makes it that much more inviting.

One particular parent held the limited idea that water was for cleaning or drinking only. But when her twins couldn't seem to get out of or past the water for other activities, she planned some acceptable water activities in an area where the water could easily be cleaned up—and they were all happy. It wasn't too long before the twins began to discover other things because they were permitted to explore one that fascinated them.

If Mom wants help with the dishes and other cleaning chores later on, she can let her preschooler help wash dishes, clean tubs and basins, wash the car or sidewalk, and bathe animals. It may take longer to finish the job and you may be anxious to complete the task yourself, but when your child is involved, he learns things about the world which will have far-reaching effects.

Water has fascinating characteristics: it is a liquid; it takes the shape of a container; it is colorless; it can be different temperatures; it can take various forms. There are so many exciting things a child can do with it! Even if he gets wet, he soon dries!

Because you spend more time with your children than do teachers, you have many opportunities to acquaint your children with the uses of water. If Mother turns the water off in her house for even a short time, she will see how many times she needs to use it. It may be hard for the preschooler to understand why the water doesn't come out of the taps when she turns them on. She then has a good opportunity to talk with the child about services in their community and the people who help with them.

How about a camping trip or a picnic? Sometimes these help you remember how dependent you are upon water and plumbing.

Suppose a faucet is leaking. As it is being repaired, you can invite the child to watch. He may have more questions than you can answer and require more time than you have, but remember that he is learning something very new and is anxious for information. As he is replacing a washer in the tap, Dad can be sure to call it by name and distinguish it from the kind of washer that is used for washing clothes. By doing so, he adds to the child's knowledge about plumbing and also to his vocabulary. How often does a teacher have as good an opportunity to help a child learn about his immediate world?

As Mom uses steam in pressing clothes, in cooking, or in cleaning, she can show the child that *this* water is very hot and takes the form of vapor or gas. She can even collect some of the moisture on a clear glass and let the child see it form to look like rain.

One caution: you must be sure that you teach true concepts to your child and that he understands them. You can give him opportunities to tell or demonstrate his knowledge without it being a performance test—listen to what he says and watch what he does. Try to help him learn about his world on *his* level and at *his* interest rate. Always be aware that you are a "facilitator of learning."

Occasionally a child asks a question that you have not anticipated and are unprepared to answer. All you need do, however, is be honest and say, "I don't know. Maybe we could look that up together." Find a book and let the child be a part of seeking the information, if possible. Most parents (and teachers) are not equipped to answer *every* question, but they can give the child confidence in parents and in books if they show him how to seek answers to his questions.

Often there is an interesting source of water in the community—a lake, a river, a pond, a fountain, a reservoir, a storage tank, or a small stream. You can take your child there, let him see these things firsthand, and then support the event with books and pictures if appropriate. It is difficult for the child to get the true perspective of a subject unless he can relate it to himself.

A child may be confused about how the sprinklers work on somebody's lawn or at the city park. Why does water spray out of the ground in some places and not in others? You can take your youngster to a place where men are laying water pipes or putting in a sprinkler system. Seeing the actual process answers many questions.

Some families are fortunate to live where water is extremely important to their livelihood—fishing, logging, boating. But their children may not know a lot about water. Parents sometimes overlook the obvious or merely assume that children know what parents know. If you have such above-mentioned opportunities readily available, be sure to use them. If they aren't available, look for good substitutes.

You are a teacher at all times. You can find many excellent opportunities to help your child learn about himself and his environment. Be careful not to bombard your child with information. Stimulate his curiosity by providing meaningful experiences that he is able to use.

Think about it, parents. How many times just today have you had water experiences which you could have used to involve and teach your preschooler?

BEAUTY 5

As goal-oriented, time-conscious adults, we take an incredible amount for granted. We assume that the sun will rise and set each day as usual, and fail to see and enjoy the first rays of the sun in the morning or the last rays at night. As shadows change the appearance of things, we go about our busy ways, forgetting to hear, see, feel, smell, and taste life. But the child does not. Whereas adults tend to label a dripping faucet as annoying, a child picks up its rhythmic splash in his play. An adult might fail to hear the sweet song of the birds while he rushes to get a job done, but a child listens and sometimes even sings with the birds. The adult who has the most profound effect on the young child has the ability to see, feel, hear, taste, and touch with a childlike attitude—he stops and watches the graceful swaying of a tree in the soft breeze or a bird in flight, or admires the ripples as they expand on a pond. Such a person is, indeed, the finest kind of teacher.

Of prime importance to the child and his appreciation of beauty is music. Often we see a preschooler bouncing up and down to the sound of a radio or TV commercial or figuring out his own dance routine to the sounds of the stereo. Rhythm is important to the child. He develops a keen sense of hearing from listening to music. He learns the names of musical selections fairly easily and requests them to be played because he enjoys listening and participating. Rather than waiting until the child becomes a teenager playing music which seems obnoxious to adult ears, the teacher should give the child early experiences with a variety of rhythms, instruments, and tone.

Music is exceptionally good as an emotional release for preschoolers. With it they sing vigorously, play instruments, use their large muscles, march, or move however they feel to the mood and the rhythm. Soft music slows their pace and fast music quickens it. Put some music on and watch! "Giving a

young child a chance to first experience rhythm in his own body movement prepares him for the more complex process of synchronizing his movement with the rhythm of someone else's sound pattern" (Landreth, 1972:104).

Color is also a strong and important part of aesthetic beauty. If young children are guided wisely in their awareness of color, they can develop a lasting appreciation for it in many aspects of their environment. The child learns to identify colors and perhaps even how to make them, but his learning doesn't end here. Color is involved in everything we do. We learn how to combine it attractively in our clothing, in our home, in our activities, and in our food. If we plan a meal in which all of the food and decor is the same color—white on a white plate on a white table cloth—will it be appetizing? We use color for emotional effect, for contrast, for accent, for variety.

Too often we do for children what they could do themselves and hence rob them of considerable growth and enjoyment. In the area of art, for example, too much of the time teachers prepare and set out materials for the children to use when the children would benefit from seeing and putting the full activity into process themselves—detail by detail, from beginning to end. They can easily mix materials, get what they need, replace materials, and clean up afterwards. Though teachers may prefer doing it, children need to learn from first-hand encounters.

Let me illustrate from my own experience with preschoolers. One group of children was very reluctant to mix paints for fear of making a mess, but when the environment was adequately prepared, they spent more time mixing paint than using it. Cleaning up was just part of the experience and they thoroughly enjoyed it. One child, excitedly anticipating his color, said, "I am going to make light blue!" He must have stayed at the paint table for a good thirty minutes before he finished. But sure enough, he had made light blue. He was extremely proud, and when the teacher asked how he had arrived at his masterpiece, he explained the procedure step by step, relating how he had tried this and then that in order to get just the right shade. And then he added with an awe-tinged sigh, "Last, I put in white!" Now he knows how to make light blue without all of the in-between steps, just as the children who have mixed other colors know how to make them. This is learning that lasts.

The ability to appreciate art and beauty is the result of experience, and adults can help children develop this ability by pointing out things of beauty in color, form, composition, and contrast.

A child's self-concept can be enhanced by his experiences with beauty. As he hears and learns to use new words, he is able to communicate what he sees, feels, hears. He becomes more secure because his knowledge increases through first-hand experiences. Small concepts merge to form larger ones.

Language is also an extremely important part of the child's understanding and enjoyment of beauty, and the teacher must be careful not to overlook it.

Talking with someone is one kind of experience. Hearing stories, poems, and songs is another. When you encourage children to express ideas and sounds, you often discover their humor and are delightfully enlightened. The effective teacher provides stimulating experiences and then listens to the conversation.

This chapter is designed to:

- Acquaint children with three aspects of his environment: music, art, and literature.
- Acquaint children with three types of instruments (woodwind, percussion, and string).
- Increase children's awareness of sound.
- Give children experience in making and using rhythm instruments.
- Give children the opportunity to find a constructive emotional release through music.
- Make music a bigger part of children's daily lives.
- Help the children learn the names and characteristics of different colors and provide an organized method of arranging colors (color wheel).

113

- Encourage children to become aware of and appreciate color in its natural form and show them how colors or dyes can be made from plants (leaves, berries, vegetables).
- Give children the opportunity to mix a variety of colors by using combinations of primary colors.
- Help children enjoy and appreciate literature.
- Give children experiences with listening and sound.
- Encourage children to use language through interacting with others, telling stories, forming words that rhyme, and enjoying themselves.
- Encourage children to use books.
- Introduce new words to the children that relate to music, art, and literature.
- Stimulate parents and other adults to provide aesthetic experiences for children.

The following three themes—Music in My Life, Give Me Color, and Books Help Me Learn—are included here to give the adult a variety of ideas and creative approaches for teaching children about things of beauty in their world.

THEME 1: MUSIC IN MY LIFE

Preassessment

- Ask the children if they know what the word *music* means.
- Ask them if they know the names of any musical instruments.
- Ask them what kind of music they like to hear.
- Ask them if they have ever played a musical instrument.
- Ask them if they have heard/seen a band or orchestra practice.
- Ask them if they know the names of different kinds of instruments:
  - those we blow into,
  - those we hit,
  - and those we pluck, strum, or play with a bow.

Behavioral Objectives

At the end of the unit, the children will be able to:

- Name three instruments and explain how they are played.
- Participate in a rhythm band.
- Attend a rehearsal of a band or an orchestra.
- When given instruments or facsimiles, place into groups those that are woodwind, those that are percussion, and those that are string.
- Demonstrate how to play at least two instruments correctly.
- Listen to records of different tempos and identify them as being fast or slow.
- Call one record or selection by name.

- Sing a simple song.
- Name three parts of a selected instrument.
- Demonstrate or define one musical term (*tempo, vibration, tone, scale*).

Evaluation

- Which of the children freely participated in the musical activities?
- Which children correctly identified the instruments in the three different groups?
- How did the children respond to using the rhythm instruments?
- If you were to teach this theme again, would you take the children to a rehearsal or have a guest or guests come to your center?
- Were the experiences too advanced for the children?
- Do some children need additional experiences with the concepts presented today?
- Which children were especially interested in the instruments?
- What would help your children most—records, instruments, a guest, singing, participating—to learn further about this topic?

- Did you notice any of the children musically or rhythmically involved at times when music was not stressed?
- Which children seem to really enjoy music? Which ones shun it?

There may be other appropriate questions. (Now you have preassessed for further teaching on the subject of music.)

Sample Lesson Plan 1

THEME: Music in My Life

Preassessment

- Ask the children if they know anyone who plays a musical instrument.
- Ask them if they know the difference between a band and an orchestra.
- Ask them if they know what the terms *woodwind, percussion,* and *string* refer to.
- Show the children pictures of various instruments and see if they can identify them.

Concepts

- We make music with different instruments.
- There are different kinds of instruments.
- There are different ways to play instruments.
- Instruments have different parts.
- We can hear music (record, TV, stereo) or we can make it (sing, play instruments, clap).
- Music makes us feel many different ways.

Behavioral Objectives

At the end of the day, the children will be able to:

- Identify from a group of instruments or facsimiles two instruments in each of the three following categories: woodwind, percussion, and string.
- Demonstrate or explain how each instrument is played.
- Participate in a rhythm activity.

Learning Activities

- Instruments, pictures, or replicas will be used.
- Guests will display, explain, and play different kinds of instruments.
- The children will have an opportunity to make and use rhythm instruments.
- Materials will be provided at the cognitive table to encourage children to explore and experiment with sound.

116

- Stories about music will be used.
- Music and props to encourage use of large muscles will be used outside.

Schedule of Activities

Review plans for the day

Check-in

Have pictures of musical instruments on the bulletin board as the children check in.

Setting the learning stage

- Review preassessment.
- Tell the children you have some friends who have come to share something with them today.
  - Introduce one friend who plays a wind instrument. Have him show it to the children, assemble it, name the basic parts, and show the children how he plays it by playing a song familiar to them. Tell them again that this is called a wind instrument because we play it by blowing into the mouthpiece.
  - Introduce another friend who plays a percussion instrument. Have him show it to the children, name the basic parts, and demonstrate how it is played. Tell them again that this is called a percussion instrument because we play it by hitting one part against another.
  - Introduce your third friend who plays a string instrument. Have him show it to the children, name the basic parts, and demonstrate how it is played by playing a song familiar to them.
  - Now have all three musicians play songs while the children sing along. As the guests leave, let the children watch as they put their instruments away, and review the terms once more.

Note: The reason for having three guests instead of one is that you are trying to set the stage for further learning about each type of instrument and must preassess. The behavioral objectives for this particular plan require that all three be taught the same day so that the children can distinguish between them. Another approach is to discuss each instrument separately and then combine them at a later date.

Free play

- Housekeeping area: provide the regular equipment. Have music playing.
- Blocks: use large and small ones, but do not emphasize.
- Creative expression: show the children how they can make musical

instruments by placing hard objects (rocks, rice, beans, seeds) in containers (paper plates stapled together, small juice containers, or rollers made from paper towels or toilet paper) covered with a durable material and secured on the ends; in round oat boxes; in 3 lb. metal cans with an elastic material stretched over the ends and secured. Cover a comb with tissue paper and hum on the teeth, or have a small box and secure rubber bands across an opening for a vibration experience. Tell the children to put their finished instruments aside for later use.

- Cognitive or science table: have pop bottles with varying amounts of water in each. Show the children how to blow across the top of each in order to produce a sound. Show the children that by changing the water level in the bottles, the notes also change. Provide a xylophone or bells for experimentation. Empty flower pots of different sizes make different tones when lightly struck by a padded mallet. (Suspend the pots on a cord or light rope with a knot in the rope inside the pot which supports it. The other end is attached to a pole or ceiling. The pots hang upside-down.)

118

- Book corner and books: see list of books on page 121.

Prestory activities

Use some of the children's favorite songs or finger plays, or just have a fun talking time until all the children arrive.

Story time

- Smith, Eunice Y. *The Little Red Drum*. Chicago: Albert Whitman & Co., 1961.
- Steiner, Charlotte. *Kiki Loves Music*. Garden City, N. Y.: Doubleday, 1949.

Music

Ask the children to bring in the instruments they made during free play. Be sure to have some extras in case some of the children didn't make any. Let the children experiment with the sounds they can make. When they settle down, put on a waltz record (or play the piano) and let the children respond to it. Then play a march and let the children respond. Have the children put their instruments away and then go to the snack.

Snack or lunch

- Encourage independence through self-service.
- Make this a relaxed period during which the children enjoy conversing and eating.

Outside activities

Take a record player outside. Give the children streamers, balloons, scarves, or other props which encourage movement to the music.

Check-out

- The children put away their props and get a learning card before departing.
- Suggested learning card:

(School or teacher's name) _____   _____ (Date) _____

Theme: Music in My Life

Today we had a fun time at school learning about music.
We had some guests who came to show us their instruments.
One played a woodwind (flute), one played a percussion (drum), and one played
a string (cello) instrument. They told us about their instruments and
showed how they play them. We made some instruments and played them.
Our teacher took a record player outside and let us move to music using streamers,
balloons, and scarves. It was so fun to run and jump with something
flying behind us. Music is very much a part of my life.

Evaluation

- Which children could name the three types of instruments and give examples of each?
- Which children could demonstrate or explain how to play each instrument?
- Were the children interested in making and using their own instruments? Give examples.
- How many of the children participated with the pop bottles, bells, and flower pots? Could they tell the difference between the tones?
- Which children asked questions of the guests?

- Did some of the children offer information about other music experiences they had had?
- Of the three types of instruments, which was the easiest for the children to understand? the most difficult?
- How could you expand upon this theme for further teaching?
- If you do not play an instrument, where can you go for resource people?
- Are you aware that you have now laid the groundwork for further teaching about instruments?
- Were there additional experiences during the day that need to be shared with other staff members?
- Which children need more time or experiences to help them clearly understand the concepts for today?

Books Available Throughout the Day

- Horwich, Frances R. *Here Comes the Band.* New York: Golden Press, 1956.
- Lacey, Marion. *Picture Book of Musical Instruments.* Boston: Lothrop, Lee, and Shepard Co., 1942.
- Ryland, Lee. *Goldon and the Glockenspiel.* Racine, Wis.: Whitman Publishing Co., 1966.
- Steiner, Charlotte. *Kiki Dances.* Garden City, N. Y.: Doubleday and Co., 1949.

    For additional aids on this theme, see page 171.

Plan for Tomorrow

THEME 2: GIVE ME COLOR

Preassessment

- Have some large pieces of paper or fabric in the three primary colors and ask the children to name the colors.
- Ask all children wearing a certain color to stand up.
- Show pictures of animals (a pink pig, a red rooster, a yellow chick, a blue jay) and see if the children can identify the animal and also the color.
- Show a real piece of fruit or vegetable and ask the children to identify the object and its color.
- Without visual aids, name a color and then ask the children to think of things at home or in the classroom that are the same color.
- Take a short walk around the vicinity and point out the various colors in nature. How do the children respond?
- Look at the hair coloring of the children and determine if they know what group they belong to (yellow, brown, black, white, red).

- Show a picture and ask the children to name as many items as they can in the picture that are the same color.
- Display many fabric samples of solid colors other than the primary colors and determine how many the children can identify.
- Show a variety of shades of the same color (light blue to navy, for example) and see if the children call them all blue or if they can attach different names for the blues.
- Ask each child to describe the colors in his own clothing and to see if anyone else in the room is wearing the same colors.

Behavioral Objectives

At the end of this experience, the children will be able to:

- Name and point to the three primary colors, the three secondary colors, and/or at least three other colors.
- When given a set of color samples (paint chips, fabric, paper), match these correctly with an additional set of color samples.
- Using powder paint and water, mix paint for use with the easel or another activity.
- Mix and explain how to make pastel colors.
- Demonstrate the combining of colors, using paint, colored cellophane, or food coloring.
- Explain how two other colors are made from mixing primary colors.
- Name the colors of objects in the room.
- Name a favorite color.
- Given the name of a color, name at least three things not in sight that are that color.
- When given several colored objects, group them into like colors.

Evaluation

- Which children already knew the names of the primary colors? Did they also know the names of the secondary colors? How many colors could they correctly identify?
- Which children had difficulty identifying the primary colors? What was the reason for this (color blindness, lack of experience, laziness)?
- Which children freely mixed colors? What were some of their comments?
- Which one of the learning activities interested the children the most? the least?
- Which children were able to match paint color samples with other paint samples or objects? Which colors were the easiest for the children to match?
- Could any of the children verbalize how they made a different color by combining two colors?

122

- What evidence did you see or hear that made you think the children were more aware of color as a result of today's activities?
- If you were to use this theme again, how would you change the plan to make it more effective?

There may be other appropriate questions. (Now you have preassessed for further teaching about color.)

Sample Lesson Plan 2

THEME: Give Me Color

Preassessment

- Show objects in the primary colors and ask the children to name the colors.
- Ask the children where we get colors.
- Describe a child's clothing by color and see if the children can guess who the child is.

123

- Ask the children if they know what primary colors are. Ask them to name them.
- Ask the children if they know what secondary colors are. Ask them to name them.

Concepts

- Each color has a name.
- Different shades of the same color have a different name.
- Colors can be made by mixing different colors.
- From the three primary colors all other colors are made.
- The primary colors are red, yellow, and blue.
- The secondary colors are orange, green, and purple. They are made by mixing the primary colors.

Behavioral Objectives

At the end of the day, the children will be able to:

124

- Name and point to the three primary colors and the three secondary colors.
- Demonstrate or explain how one of the secondary colors is made from the primary colors.
- Name three objects in the room that are primary and secondary colors.

Learning Activities

- Games, songs, and musical activities involving color will be used.
- Color in various forms (paper, food coloring, paint, fabrics) will be available for mixing and comparing.
- Names and examples of the primary, secondary, and other colors will be used freely by teachers.
- Children will have the opportunity to place things of like color into different groups.
- A food experience during free play will be provided.
- Books involving color will be placed in the book corner. Appropriate stories will be used.

- A science experience will be provided.
- Outside activities will involve large muscles and color.

Schedule of Activities

Review plans for the day

Check-in

As each child enters and is greeted, the teacher can make comments about the color scheme of the child's clothing. The teacher can also relate some of the colors to the school setting or other children.

Setting the learning stage
- Review preassessment.
- Show different objects and have the children name the color of each (orange carrot, blue feather, purple plum, red flower). Use some objects that can be more than one color—an apple can be green, red, yellow. Use some objects that are always the same color.
- Introduce the primary colors by name and example.
- Introduce the secondary colors by name and example.
- Show a color wheel and explain how the colors are arranged on it.

Free play
- Housekeeping area: provide large mirrors and large pieces of fabrics so that the children can see how they look in different colors.
- Food experience: make different colors of gelatin dessert for snack or lunch.
- Blocks: supply small, colored, plastic cubes of matching color for building.
- Creative area: have undiluted food coloring in primary colors and put each primary color in one egg section of a white foam egg carton. Have a small jar of water and an eye dropper for each child. Put a small amount of water in the remaining egg sections. Encourage the children to mix colors by taking drops of the primary colors and putting them into the water. When the children finish mixing the colors, they can pour them out and start over again. Let the children mix paint to use at the easel or for painting wood scraps. Use large, unwaxed paper plates and have scraps of tissue cut so the children can stick them on the plates with liquid starch rather than paste.
- Manipulative area: use brightly colored puzzles or colored shapes and form boards.
- Cognitive or sensory table: provide a variety of colored objects made from different materials (fabric, wood, metal) for exploratory, sensory experiences.

126

- Book corner and books: see list of books on page 129.

Prestory activities

Provide a science experience for the children. Have a hot plate, water, and pans ready. Show the children how color can be made by boiling different items: vegetables (carrots, beets, spinach), leaves (make green or brown), berries (make red or purple), or paper (makes many colors). After doing this, put pieces of white fabric in the colored solutions. Take some out quickly and let others remain in order to get different shades. Macaroni pieces can be put into liquid food coloring and used in creative activities another day. Put the macaroni on paper towels to drain and then on waxed paper to dry.

Story time

- Baum, Arline, and Joseph. *One Bright Monday Morning.* New York: Random House, 1962.
- Bright, Robert. *I Like Red.* Garden City, N. Y.: Doubleday and Co., 1955.

127

Music

- Records: Kimbo Educational Records, P.O. Box 246, Dial, N.J. 07723
  "Parade of Color," #EA522
  "Color," #ARLP-514

Note: As the children leave the story and music activities today, try a new technique. Instead of all the children going at once to have their snack, suggest that all those wearing a certain color go first, then another color go next, and so on. In this way the children go to snack in spaced groups and the theme is reinforced.

Snack or lunch

- Eat the gelatin prepared during free play.

Outside activities

- The teacher can take a walk with the children around the school area, pointing out the colorful things in nature or in man-made objects.
- Large cardboard boxes can be provided for the children to paint.

Check-out

- The children return their toys and get a learning card before they depart.
- Suggested learning card:

(School or teacher's name) _____   _____ (Date) _____

Theme: Color

Today we talked about color and learned that every color has a name. The three colors from which all other colors are made are red, yellow, and blue. They are called primary colors. From mixing two of the primary colors, orange, green, and purple are made. These are called secondary colors.
All other colors are made from mixing primary and secondary colors.
We had many experiences with color today, including mixing colors, playing games, singing and moving to music, preparing food, and talking with each other.

Evaluation

- Which children could name and point to the primary and secondary colors?
- How many of the children participated in the creative experiences?

- Which of the learning activities interested the children the most? the least?
- Were any of the children confused about the mixing of secondary colors?
- Are some of the children color-blind?
- Are some of the children still having trouble distinguishing one color from another?
- What additional experiences could you provide which would help the children further their understanding about color?

Books Available Throughout the Day

- Anglund, Joan W. *What Color Is Love?* New York: Harcourt, Brace and World, 1966.
- Burton, Virginia Lee. *The Little House.* Boston: Houghton Mifflin, 1942.
- Freeman, Don. *A Rainbow of My Own.* New York: Viking Press, 1966.
- McDonald, Golden. *Red Light, Green Light.* Garden City, N. Y.: Doubleday and Co., 1944.
- Rothschild, Alice. *Fruit Is Ripe for Timothy.* New York: Young Scott Books, 1963.
- Scott, Rachelle. *Colors, Colors All Around.* New York: Grosset & Dunlap.
- Tripp, Paul. *The Little Red Flower.* Garden City, N. Y.: Doubleday and Co., 1968.

For additional aids on this theme, see pages 171-173.

Plan for Tomorrow

THEME 3: BOOKS HELP ME LEARN

Preassessment

- Whisper instructions to the children and see how many follow through.
- Ask them what they like to do at school (hopefully some of them will mention things which require verbal language).
- Ask them what they would do if they couldn't hear.
- Ask them if they like to hear stories, poetry, and songs.
- Ask them what someone said to them today that made them happy.
- Ask them to tell something they like to do.
- Ask them why we have books.
- Ask them how many want to learn to read. Why?
- Ask them if they know how to write their names. Can they write anything else?
- Ask them if they have ever made up a story, poem, or song.
- Ask them what words they like to say. Can they make up new words?
- Ask them to tell you what they would like to be when they grow up.

Behavioral Objectives

At the end of the unit, the child will be able to:

● Give two reasons why we have books.
● Individually or with a group assist in making up a story, a poem, or a song.
● Explain something to another person.
● Make a picture, explaining it to a teacher so the story or information can be written on it.
● Show and tell his favorite story.
● Record a conversation and then play it back.

Evaluation

● Which children spend time looking at books during the day? Are there some who never look at books?
● What reasons did they give for having books?
● Did all the children participate in creating a story, a poem, or a song?
● When given specific instructions to convey to another person, which children could do it accurately?
● Which children participated in the creative activities? Could they give a verbal description about their pictures?
● Name the favorite stories mentioned by some of the children. Are these stories they have heard at school? Do some books seem to be favorites with many of the children? What themes do the children seem to like most?
● Were the children interested in hearing records or tape recorders?
● What were some of the more creative statements the children made during the day?
● Do some of the children seldom or never verbally communicate with others?
● Do some of the children use physical methods (hitting, shoving, or grabbing) to get what they want rather than verbal ones? If so, how can you assist these children?
● Is it important for children to learn to listen as well as to speak?
● Does the child's verbal ability reflect how he feels about himself?

There may be other appropriate questions. (Now you have preassessed for further teaching about books.)

Sample Lesson Plan 3

THEME: Books Help Me Learn

Preassessment

● Ask the children if they know how we can find information about things.
● Ask them where we get books. Do they know anyone who can read?

- Ask them if they have heard themselves talk.
- Ask them what kind of books they like.
- Ask them if they know what a poem is.
- Ask them if they have ever made up a story, a poem, or a song.

Concepts

- We learn by reading books and looking at the pictures.
- It is fun to hear stories, poems, and songs.
- There are two ways to communicate: talking (verbal) and reading (written symbols). Clarify these terms for the children. (When you talk to people, they usually know what you want. When you don't, they usually don't know what you want.)
- We learn through seeing and hearing.

Behavioral Objectives

At the end of the day, the children will be able to:

- Give two reasons why we have books.
- Record and play back their conversations or other sounds.
- Describe something they have done or made so the teacher can record the information.
- State some rhyming words.
- Using visual aids, tell a story (original or retold).

Learning Activities

- Use a tape recorder.
- Talk to the children about the importance of books.
- Provide activities in which children can verbalize (telling stories, talking about their work, participating in groups).
- Encourage children to use verbal communication as they work and play. Help them think of rhyming or descriptive terms.

Schedule of Activities

Review plans for the day

Check-in

Record a verbal greeting with each child.

Setting the learning stage

- Review preassessment.
- Play the tape you recorded as the children came today.

- Show a favorite book of the children and ask them to tell you something about it.
- Use a few good poems. Ask the children what a poem is. Help them make up rhyming words.
- Stimulate language throughout the day.

Free play

- Housekeeping area: rather than use them in the regular way, have some flannel boards and visual aids today so the children can tell stories.
- Blocks: have a record player set up and set out some favorite records the children can use.
- Creative expression: get some of the most exciting raw materials you can think of (lace, shells, glitter, seeds, paint) and encourage the children to make pictures with them. Ask them to discuss their pictures with you. Write on each picture the description the children give you. Writing is another way of explaining pictures. Use the easel with bright paper and some new colors. Write about these, too.
- Manipulative area: provide woodworking tools, wood, and paint.
- Cognitive or science table: have the tape recorder here. Let the children record their voices and other sounds and then play them back.
- Book corner and books: use favorites of the children.

Prestory activity

Let the children help make up a story. To add interest you could quickly make some sketches (stick figures if you like) on a low bulletin board or large sheet of paper. Encourage each child to participate. Stories like this are usually different and take sudden changes.

Story time

- Use stories in which children can participate, for example:
Slobodkina, Esphyr. *Caps for Sale.* New York: Wm. R. Scott, 1947.
- Or build a story around a finger play or song such as "Johnny Works," p. 26, Smith, R., and Charles Leonhard. *Discovering Music Together.* Chicago: Follett Publishing Co., 1968.

Music

Today play a short classical record just for listening.

Snack or lunch

Nothing special is served, but the children are still encouraged to serve themselves and remove their dishes.

Outside activities

Use the regular equipment but organize it in a different manner to stimulate the interest and use of the children.

Check-out

- The children are encouraged to replace their equipment and get a learning card before they depart.
- Suggested learning card:

(School or teacher's name)	(Date)

Theme: Books Help Me Learn

Language is important to me. I can learn by hearing spoken language, and
    someday I will be able to read written words. Books help me understand
    my world because I can look at the pictures and someone can read the writing
    to me. I like to hear stories and poems.
We did some fun things with language today. We heard our voices on a tape
    recorder, helped make up a story, and told our teacher about the things we
    did so she could write about them.
When we do interesting things, we have something exciting to talk about.

Evaluation

- Which children could explain why we have books?
- Were any of the children reluctant to use the tape recorder?
- Which children described their work for a teacher to record? Were any hesitant?
- Did you hear the children using language in a novel way today (making up rhyming words, new descriptions)?
- Which children used the visual aids to tell stories?
- Which children need more experience in verbalizing?
- Did the children seem to understand the importance of communicating?
- Did any of the children enjoy looking at books by themselves?

Books Available Throughout the Day

Have a good variety of familiar books rather than introduce new ones today.
For additional aids on this theme, see page 173.

Plan for Tomorrow

133

ESPECIALLY FOR PARENTS

Parents exert an extremely powerful influence on their children's attitudes toward beauty, especially in the areas of music, art, and literature. You need make only one negative remark ("Music is only for sissies!" Or "Reading is dumb!") and your preschooler usually acquires the same attitude, often even parroting the same phrases to his peers.

If you enjoy the arts, your children will usually enjoy them. Take your children to concerts, art museums, and libraries and let them enjoy and share pleasant moments with you. Teach by positive example. If you force your child to sit quietly through a concert when you are unable to do so, you will most likely give your child a negative attitude toward that which could be thoroughly enjoyable.

Many people fill their leisure time with music, art, or literature, using them for enjoyment, emotional release, and general satisfaction. Such acceptable outlets enrich and beautify life.

About music

If you have had training in vocal or instrumental music, you can help your children benefit from the same experiences. If you have no such background, at least give your children a chance to enjoy these and let them decide whether they like them. No matter what your background, all you need do is watch your preschoolers participate in a musical activity to realize that it is very important to them.

Children enjoy the rhythmical beat of music, and participation with it helps them develop their coordination. Many of their other activities also involve rhythm (running, pounding, swinging).

Parents can provide many kinds of musical experience for their young children. Preschoolers enjoy soft singing while they are being held and rocked. They stop their play to listen to a catchy jingle on the radio or television. They take special note when a band marches by in a parade. They especially enjoy the independence of playing their own instruments (even lids and spoons from the cupboard) or using a record player they can manipulate. They excitedly sit on the piano stool by an adult who plays as they both sing familiar songs. They marvel as a sibling practices his music.

Musical experiences are very pleasant for the young child unless he is made to sit for long periods of time or in an uncomfortable seat to listen to someone display advanced skills. If the anxious parent waits until the child has developed enough control over his body so that he can sit still and listen, the child will very likely develop a positive, rather than a negative, attitude toward music.

Many times during the day you and your child can enjoy a musical sound, rhythm, or other movement activity together—a bird's song, music playing

while you are working or playing, sounds made by transportation vehicles (the fog horn of a boat, the whistle of a train, or the roar of an airplane), sounds within the home (phone ringing, clock ticking, children laughing), the movement of the trees in the soft breeze, the rustle of leaves or clothes flapping on the clothesline, the sound of daddy's feet approaching the door. Many of these experiences, which most adults take for granted, provide excellent learning moments for the small child.

Rather than just relying on a musical moment occurring without any personal effort, look for special kinds of experiences which are interesting to preschoolers. Mom or Dad (or both) can take the child to a music store, to a nearby friend who plays an instrument, to a local school or dance studio when a class is in session. As a result, the child will learn to love and appreciate good music.

When children have been especially aggressive and tense, play a quiet, soothing record or a quiet, pleasant piece on the piano, and your children will pick up the calm mood. Likewise, lethargic children become vigorous when they listen to a musical selection that has a definite, fast rhythm. Many parents have discovered they can actually change the pace of their children with the use of such music. Adults are also susceptible; for this reason store managers play soft, quiet music as we shop. They want us to slow down and spend our money.

Children enjoy the physical release they get when actively participating with a lively record or with a rhythm experience. We need to help them discover activities which allow them such releases for their frustrations. Preschoolers must learn that it is acceptable to pound a drum, but not a sibling; it is acceptable to jump and run in the backyard, but not on the furniture.

Many children who do master a musical instrument or physical expression to music (such as dancing) find satisfaction in displaying their skills. They form healthy attitudes early and desire to hear good music and participate in it.

About color

You can help young children learn about color in many ways—most of the time in a rather casual on-the-spot type of interaction, but also with some degree of preplanning.

If you decorate the child's room and buy his clothes and toys, make a deliberate attempt to provide an environment that is pleasing and colorful, as well as stimulating and harmonious.

As the child begins to develop and use an understandable verbal language, casually say in talking to him, "This is a red ball," rather than "This is a ball." In this way, you can add color to the child's understanding of the object and help him increase his language, his concepts, and his ability to discriminate between colors.

Suppose it is your particular preschooler's birthday. You can tell him that a shirt or dress of his choice is to be a special present. And then rather than let the child select obnoxious garments, help him select several which are appropriate and let him make the final selection. "Here is a blue one, or a red one, or a green one. Which one of these do you like?" Again, you are helping your child become aware of color while also giving him the opportunity to make a selection, both of which are necessary to the child's development. When you place confidence in his choice, he feels important. If you let him select from the entire store and he chooses something you don't like, however, you will very likely end up in a power struggle.

You do not always have to select books which have colorful illustrations. More important than color is the clearness of the representations. Though a book may contain colorful illustrations which are pleasing to look at, its story may not be as good as that of a book with black and white pictures. Children have favorites which are illustrated in black and white, bronze and white, or one color and white.

While a parent should not focus too strongly on color, he should help the child look for and appreciate color in his environment. For example, Dad and his preschooler are going to the grocery store. Rather than letting his child drift off to the cereal or candy section (which are really favorites), he encourages him to accompany him to the produce section. As Dad selects fruits and vegetables, he tells the child what to look for—lettuce should be firm and green, tomatoes should be firm and red (soft ones are often over-ripe and will mash or spoil easily), and so on down the counter. Sometimes we purchase fruit which is green and allow it to ripen at home before eating it (bananas, pears, peaches). As they ripen, they change color. Generally the produce which has the most brilliant color is ready to eat and is the most palatable.

As Dad passes the canned goods section, he points out that each can has a picture of the contents on it so that he can tell if he is buying green string beans or yellow wax beans, for example. He can read the label, but the picture helps. When he gets to the section which has puddings, gelatin, cake mixes, frosting, Dad tells his child that he needs two packages of green gelatin and two

137

of red, some yellow or brown pudding, or a white cake mix, and lets the child select these items. The child may take a little time at first, but the experience is one which he will build on forever.

When you buy ice cream, how does your child tell you what kind he wants? He names the color: "I want pink!" All you need to do is explain: "They have strawberry pink, cherry pink, and mint pink. Show me which pink you mean." Then help him identify the color with a flavor.

Sometimes parents make requests of children but fail to give them enough information. For instance, "Go and get Dad's shoes, please." The child brings back a pair that Daddy doesn't want. But if you say, "Go and get Daddy's white shoes with the blue shoe laces," your child will more than likely be able to complete the task successfully. "Bring me that book" is a very vague request. "Bring me the yellow book that has a picture of a dog on it over there on the blue table" is concrete—and a winner for the child!

Suppose you have small wooden objects in the primary colors and in three shapes (circles, squares, and triangles). Ask your child to put all of those that are alike in one pile. Just for the sake of our color concepts, let's say he sorts them into piles of red, yellow, and blue. Good job! Now ask him if he can put those that are alike into piles other than by color. He may be able to sort them by shape, for example, or be puzzled until one gets him thinking about shape. This exercise helps him to see that color is only one way of sorting things (or shape, if that is his first way of sorting). As he understands these two means of categorizing, you can then introduce another dimension—as he indicates his readiness—such as large and small sizes in each shape, or additional colors with a larger variety of shapes.

An inexpensive bottle of bubble-blowing solution can bring hours of enjoyment to a child and also teach him valuable concepts about his environment. Help him identify the colors present in the bubbles, notice the reflections on the bubbles, explain that air is enclosed within each bubble.

You do not have to spend a great deal of money in order to give your children good color experiences. Everywhere we look, we see color! Teaching situations are not isolated from everyday life; they are integrated with it. How much more valuable are these experiences to the preschooler than a box of crayons, for example, from which we ask him to learn the colors just so he can tell them by name.

About literature

Children notice if their parents spend time reading and also what they read (newspapers, books, letters, magazines) and develop similar attitudes toward reading. Children who do not see their parents reading often do not read either. Some children spend most of their waking hours looking at books. Both extremes need to arrive at a happy medium.

One of the most pleasant times of day in some households (whether bedtime, a quiet break from the daily routine, or another time) is when Mom or Dad sits down with a youngster and cuddles him close to read a book. This is a precious time which only they share. Maybe it is the closeness of someone else. Maybe it is the book being read. Maybe it is the relaxation. Whatever it is that makes it so enjoyable, reading with someone the child loves and trusts is special.

After a young child learns ideas from books, these ideas become really meaningful if they are supported by firsthand experiences. Books most appropriate for young children should, therefore, contain experiences the child could have himself (Arbuthnot, 1972; Read, 1971). Until a child is in the operational stage (ages 7-11), he is not able to consistently think in abstract terms (Piaget, 1966). In other words, the child is egocentric (thinking of things from his own point of view) and deals in the here-and-now. Stories containing abstract ideas, unrealistic information, and advanced concepts confuse the preschooler and are best used with school-age children.

A very delightful experience for you and your preschooler can be a periodic trip to the local library or to a nearby school to check out books. Sometimes, one chooses books for rather different, interesting reasons (the child likes the color of the cover or the parent selects one of his old favorites, forgetting at what age he enjoyed it). However, what is most important is that they enjoy sharing the experience.

Children often enjoy spending time alone, quietly looking at books. Perhaps the preschooler has a question about a picture that he must ask Dad, or perhaps he can pretend to read the book to a toy or a pet.

Take advantage of the perennial Mother Goose rhymes. They are full of fun words and delightful rhymes and can be used so spontaneously that they are appropriate at any time.

Preschoolers love poetry that they can understand, and many such poems are available for them. (For references, see Barbara J. Taylor, *A Child Goes Forth*. Provo, Utah: Brigham Young University Press, 1970, p. 98; or ask the local children's librarian.) Poems are another means of expressing ideas and children's poems are short, revealing ideas from a child's point of view. Once you start using them, you will be a dedicated fan—they are so delightful. Such poetry adds an extra dimension to the child's whole idea of literature and increases his awareness of and ability to enjoy beauty in another of its numerous, varied forms.

PARTS AND THE WHOLE 6

Chapters two through four have dealt with somewhat isolated topics, each important and serving a particular need. In this chapter, however, we will be dealing with how learning occurs—from the known to the unknown, from simple to complex, and from general to specific. The purpose of this final chapter is to explain how topics are related and how difficult it is to teach one idea in isolation. Though the previous chapters can be used as separate topics, they are also parts of a broader, more complex topic.

As children grasp the meaning of simple concepts and topics, we try to extend these to a broader subject area. In other words, we try to help the child see how various entities in his environment fit together as well as exist as single, distinct parts. We also use different labels for items when they are parts than when they are combined into one object. Children need to understand this.

Quite often when we attempt to think on a child's level, we find it difficult, for we realize that we have forgotten how few experiences we had or how limited our vocabulary was when we were but preschool children. It is very important then for us to be aware of information that we too often take for granted. If children are to learn accurately from adults, signals must be clear and complete, for children ofttimes form misconceptions or no concepts at all from a well-intentioned parent or teacher.

If you teach the preschooler, you must be able to help him take the pieces of a puzzle (each piece taken from the previous chapters and themes) and fit them together so that they form a logical pattern in his learning process.

This chapter is designed to:

- Help children increase their vocabulary and stimulate them to use it by learning the proper names of parts and objects.

- Better acquaint the children with everyday ideas and objects (egg, shoe, body, apple).
- Emphasize that the same name may apply to parts of a number of different objects (tongues, hammers, brushes, airplanes, fish).
- Demonstrate to the children that even though parts make up an object (door, mouth, apple, coat), that object is a part of a larger object (house, face, applesauce, clothing). This is called class inclusion.
- Help them identify the whole object by giving them a number of specific clues (many plants have roots, stems, and leaves, but the blossom distinguishes it as a flower; many objects have a handle, but the additional part [blade, tines, or scoop] distinguishes it as a knife, fork, or shovel).
- Stimulate them to explore or ask about how an object can be divided into parts (or how parts are combined to make a whole object) and also ask the names of the parts and the whole object.
- Give them experiences in and practice with classifying ideas and objects.
- Increase their awareness of their world by helping them integrate ideas and material through firsthand experiences.
- Provide a model to aid you in preparing a unit about this topic for your young children.
- Suggest some ways that you can use materials and activities in teaching children in the home.

The following two themes, It Takes Parts, and I Learn About Classification, offer you ideas for helping children form logical ideas about their world and how its many parts are integrated.

THEME 1: IT TAKES PARTS

Preassessment

- Ask the children what the words *part* and *whole* mean.
- Cut an apple in half and see if the children can name its parts (skin, meat, core, seeds, stem).
- Bring in a wagon. Discuss with the children what color it is, what can be done with it, and so on. Then ask them to name as many parts of it as they can. (Or bring in another common object, such as a doll, a plant, or a shoe.)
- Bring in the ingredients for creative material (such as fingerpaints or salt-flour dough) and see if the children can identify them. Then let them mix the material and see if they know what it is called when all ingredients are mixed together.
- Show the children a doll and let them identify the various parts. Then article by article, dress it, having the children name the articles. Tell them the name of the whole object *(doll)*, and all of the articles combined, which are required to dress it *(clothing)*.

142

- Show the children an incomplete object (toy, puzzle, vehicle) and ask them how they can use it with the part missing.
- Ask the children how many things they know that have a tongue (chances are they will name people and animals rather than objects—wagons, shoes).

Behavioral Objectives

At the end of this experience, the child will be able to:

- Identify by name the parts of several objects which have more than two parts. Also name the whole object.
- Upon presentation of visual and/or verbal clues, name the whole object.
- When given actual parts, assemble them into a whole object.

Evaluation

- Which children seemed to know the most about parts and wholes at the beginning of the day? Were these children also the ones who seemed to know the most about them at the end of the day? Use specific examples.

143

- Which children were the most verbal about the theme?
- Which of the learning activities interested the children the most? the least?
- Were any of the children relating parts and wholes in a manner different from what you had anticipated?
- Which children used new terms? Were their uses accurate?

There may be other appropriate questions. (Now you have preassessed for further teaching about the relationship between parts and the whole.

Sample Lesson Plan 1

THEME: It Takes Parts

Preassessment

- Ask the children what the words *part* and *whole* mean.
- Show the children pictures in which important parts are missing (body without one of its parts, airplane without a wing, tricycle without handlebars) and ask them what is wrong with the picture.
- Show the children some parts and see if they can identify them by name. Then combine the parts and see if the children can name the completed object.

Concepts

- Most objects have more than one part.
- Each part has a name.
- When all the parts are combined, the new object has a name different from the names of the individual parts.
- When the parts are combined into one object, they are more useful than when the parts are used alone.
- Any whole object is usually a part of an even larger unit.
- A whole object may be divided into parts.
- Some objects are in one piece which cannot be taken apart, but they still have different parts (a bottle has a neck, a body, and a base).

Behavioral Objectives

At the end of this experience, the children will be able to:

- Identify by name the parts of several objects which have more than two parts. They will also name the whole object.
- Demonstrate how the whole object is used.
- Take a simple, whole object, disassemble, and reassemble it, calling each part by name.

144

- When given a whole object, explain how it is only a part of a still larger object or unit.
- Name objects which appear to contain a single part (ball, bottle, rock, seed).

Learning Activities
- The bulletin board will contain pictures of parts of objects and also a whole object assembled from these parts or objects.
- Manipulative toys which have parts will be used (pegboards, puzzles).
- Actual objects will be used, where possible, to demonstrate the various parts they contain (picture will be used where actual objects are not practical or available).
- The children will use materials in their play which have parts (clothing, dishes).
- The children will have further firsthand experiences with parts by mixing paint for use on the easel, making salt-flour clay, and making cookies.
- A table will be provided so that the children can manipulate parts of objects to make whole objects in either the conventional way or a novel way.
- A Think Box will stimulate children to put parts together abstractly without manipulating the parts.
- A music activity will involve the whole body.
- Equipment which requires parts and cooperation will be used outside (boards and boxes, shovels and buckets, teeter-totter).

Schedule of Activities

Review plans

Check-in

Check-in time is flexible and a few books, puzzles, and pegboards are provided for the children until all the children arrive.

Setting the learning stage
- Review preassessment.
- Show parts of a small object, perhaps a toy. Describe what you have—wheels, a block of wood, and a steering wheel, for example—and ask the children to identify the parts. Then put the object together and ask the children what it is called when it is assembled.
- Define the words *parts* and *whole*. Give one or two more demonstrations until you are sure the children have the correct concepts.
- Where possible, use real objects; where not, use good visual aids.
- See Suggested Verbalization or Ideas (p. 174).

145

Free play

- Housekeeping area: set the table and provide pans and utensils for cooking. Use clothing for dramatic play.
- Food experience: let the children measure, make, and bake cookies or bread, or prepare some other food for lunch.
- Block area: provide small unit blocks.
- Creative materials: supply powder paint, water, jars and brushes so children can mix their own paint for use on the easel. Have collage materials available for cutting and pasting. Supply ingredients from which the children can make salt-flour clay.
- Sensory table: use the sand table with small farm animals and equipment (tractor, truck, plow).
- Cognitive table: supply actual parts to various objects which the children can put together (handle and head for a hammer; parts of rubber or wooden animals, toys, puzzles, rattles).
- Book corner and books: see list of books on page 150.

146

Prestory activities

- Finger plays: begin with one or two familiar finger plays to gain the attention of the children.
- Think Box: introduce the Think Box in an appealing manner. You might say, "What do you think I have in this box?" and entertain the ideas submitted by the children. Using an object that has several parts, take the parts out one by one, talking about them with the children, naming the parts, and asking the children what they think you could make with the parts. Try to select an object that will stimulate the curiosity of the children. When you have taken all of the parts from the box, get suggestions from the children as to how you might assemble them to make an object. As the object becomes more complete, discover that you need one key part and ask the children, "What do we need to finish this?" The children will suggest it, and then you get it from the box and complete the object. (Make sure you select a place for this activity which will allow for all of the children to see and be involved.)

147

Story time

- Jackson, Kathryn. *Wheels.* New York: Simon & Schuster, 1952.
- Burton, Virginia Lee. *The Little House.* New York: Houghton Mifflin, 1942.
- *Or* make a flannel board or flip-card story from the information in Suggested Verbalization or Ideas (p. 174).

Music

- "Hokey Pokey" (use record) Hollywood: MacGregor #6995 or see your local record dealer.
- Sing "Head, Shoulders, Knees, and Toes."

Snack or lunch

- Serve the cookies or other food made earlier in the day.
- Encourage the children to pour their own milk or juice, serve themselves, and remove their own dishes after eating.

Outside activities

- Have buckets and shovels placed in the sand.
- Have wheel toys such as trikes, wagons, and wheelbarrows ready.
- Arrange large climbing apparatus such as jungle gym, boards and boxes, and ramp for large muscle development.

Check-out

- Children put away their outdoor toys and get a learning card before leaving.
- Suggested learning card:

(School or teacher's name)   (Date)

Theme: Parts

Today we talked about combining parts to make a whole object. Each part has a name and the whole object has a name different from the parts. The whole object (combined parts) is more useful than when the parts are used alone.

We mixed our own creative materials, assembled various parts into whole objects, participated in a music experience using the whole body, and prepared food.

This card is merely informative. Perhaps you will find an opportune time to help your child see objects within the home and neighborhood that have parts which are combined to make larger objects or units.

Evaluation

- Which children seemed to know the most about parts and wholes at the beginning of the day? Were these children also the ones who seemed to know the most about these concepts at the end of the day? Use specific examples.
- Could most of the children name the individual parts of objects and then the name of the whole?
- What comments did the children make during the day related to the theme? Were these comments negative or positive? Why?
- If you were to use this theme again, how would you change the plan to make it more effective?
- Were the children more aware than previously of objects having parts? Use examples.
- Did the children respond comfortably to this theme and the activities, or did they seem confused? In other words, were the activities and concepts appropriate for their level of understanding?

Books Available Throughout the Day

Some can support the theme and others be a diversion from it.

- *Baum, Arline, and Joseph. *One Bright Monday Morning.* New York: Random House, 1962.
- Berends, Polly B. *Who's That in the Mirror?* New York: Random House, 1968.
- Bright, Robert. *I Like Red.* Garden City, N. J.: Doubleday and Co., 1955.
- *Brown, Margaret Wise. *The Important Book.* New York: Harper & Bros., 1949.
- Brown, Myra B. *First Night Away from Home.* Chicago: Children's Press.
- *Burton, Virginia Lee. *The Little House.* Boston: Houghton Mifflin Co.
- Taylor, Barbara J. *I Can Do.* Provo, Utah: Brigham Young University Press, 1972.

   *These books support the theme.

   For additional aids on this theme, see pages 174-175.

Plan for Tomorrow

THEME 2—I LEARN ABOUT CLASSIFICATION

Preassessment, behavioral objectives, and evaluation are somewhat limited for the area of classification, thus the section as provided in preceding chapters is eliminated here and a specific lesson plan only is considered. See pages 7-17.

Sample Lesson Plan 2

THEME: I Learn about Classification

Preassessment

- What does classification mean? (Do the children know why or how things are put into classes?)
- Name a classification (fruit, for example) and ask the children to name the kinds of fruit they know.
- Show different pictures on the same piece of paper (for example, 6 boys and 4 girls) and ask the children, "Are there more boys in this picture or more children?" Then reverse the question, "Are there more girls in this picture or more children?" Use another picture (2 butterflies and 6 birds) and ask, "Are there more birds or more things that fly in this picture?" Reverse the question. What you are trying to determine here is whether the children can classify objects into a larger category. This is one of Piaget's tasks termed classification.

150

Concepts

- Each object has a name. When it is added to other objects which are similar to it, the group has a different name. This process is called classification.
- Many objects can be called by more than one name.
- There are different ways of putting objects into groups.

Behavioral Objectives

At the end of this experience, the children will be able to:

- Name two general categories, and place the appropriate objects within them when given a number of objects.
- Give the two names (individual and group) for any two given objects.
- When given a group of objects, categorize them in at least two different ways.

Learning Activities

- A picture exercise to see how well the children respond will be used.
- Throughout the day opportunities to classify different kinds of things into a variety of groups will be provided.
- A food experience will permit children to combine ingredients.
- Spontaneous conversation throughout the day will be provided for.

Schedule of Activities

Review plans for the day

Check-in

Have books available for the children to browse through until all the children arrive.

Setting the learning stage

- Review preassessment.
- Have a number of objects on a low table, such as different kinds of vehicles, fruits, vegetables, and articles of clothing. Ask the children if they know how these things "go together." If so, let them classify them; if not, talk about each object and how it can be put into a pile or group of other similar objects. After the objects are placed in groups, ask the children if there is another way they can put them into groups (edible, color, and so on).
- Try the above classification activities with different groups of objects (flowers, animals, or airplanes, for example).
- Tell the children some of the activities that are planned for the day.

151

Free play

- Housekeeping area: have plastic or real fruits and vegetables for the children to handle and discuss. Provide other domestic items.
- Food experience: have fresh fruits that the children can peel and combine to make a fruit salad. Talk about the individual fruits, their color, how the covering is removed, and what they taste like.
- Blocks: set out a pacer, but do not emphasize this area today.
- Creative expression: set out sheets of white construction or butcher paper. In salt shakers mix salt and dry tempera. With a small brush, apply paste to the paper. Sprinkle the colored salt over the paste.
- Cognitive table: have many empty cans, boxes, or bottles which have pictures of food on them. Help the children separate them into their proper groups (fruit, vegetable, cereal). Then see if there is another way these same things can be separated into other meaningful groups. Cover three to four tables with butcher paper (or use large sheets of paper on the floor or make a large mural) and in the corner of each sheet paste one picture (food, animal, clothing, transportation). Give the children magazines and let them cut out pictures that belong to that group and paste them on the sheets.
- Book corner and books: use a variety of books available in your library.

Prestory activities

Use colorful pictures to accompany nursery rhymes. Let the children select the rhymes they want to say and then let them take turns holding up the pictures.

Story time

As it is difficult to find a story to support this theme, try a diversion story today.

- McClosky, Robert. *Blueberries for Sal.* New York: Viking Press, 1948.
- Zion, Gene. *Really Spring.* New York: Harper & Bros.

Music

Play a record which has a medium or slow tempo but no voice. Let the children take turns being a leader. Whatever the child does, the rest of the children are to imitate. This is a fun experience and doesn't put pressure upon a child to perform, because whatever he does is all right.

Snack or lunch

- Provide the necessary ingredients (bread, butter, and filling) and let each child make himself a sandwich.
- Also serve the fruit salad the children prepared earlier in the day.

152

Outside activities

- Take large wooden boards and boxes and make a new arrangement. If possible, get large cardboard boxes used for shipping refrigerators, washers, and other large equipment and cut holes in them to represent doors and/or windows. Let the children arrange them for dramatic play.
- Have toys and equipment in the sand area.

Check-out

- Help the children put their toys away and get a learning card before departing.
- Suggested learning card:

(School or teacher's name) _____   _____ (Date) _____

Theme: I Learn about Classification

Today we had experiences in classifying objects into different groups. We
learned that each object has a name; but when it is added to other similar
objects, it has a different name (for example, a dog is also an animal).
For our snack, we made a fruit salad and our own sandwiches from
combining different items of food. After we had grouped items, we
tried to see if there was another way they could be grouped (an apple
is a fruit, but it can also be edible, and has a particular color).

Evaluation

- Which children were able to grasp the concept of classification? Which children were not able to?
- Was it difficult for the children to understand that an object can be called by different terms?
- Which children could group objects in more than one way?
- Were the children frustrated by the activities today? Were the concepts too advanced?
- If you were to use this same theme again, how would you change your plan to make it more effective for your particular children?
- Do some children need more experience with these concepts in order to understand them?
- Are some children ready for more advanced experiences in classification?
- How did you feel about the concepts and experiences today?
- Which classification activities did the children enjoy the most? the least? Why?

153

Books Available Throughout the Day

Use familiar books or introduce new ones for the children's enjoyment. For additional aids on this theme, see page 175.

Plan for Tomorrow

ESPECIALLY FOR PARENTS

Perhaps parents wonder why they should spend time and effort helping their children learn how smaller objects or ideas fit into a child's world. But actually you lay the groundwork for integrating the many segments of your child's life. As "no man is an island," no topic exists in and of itself, for it is directly or indirectly connected with many other topics. For example, when you teach your child music, you also teach him sound, muscle development, attitudes, rhythm, and motion, along with other things.

Actually, classification is necessary for concept formation. We give entities names, we relate unknowns to knowns, we show relationships, and we advance from general to specific information.

Parents can share many daily experiences with their children—let them put away the groceries, separate the fruit from the vegetables or boxes from cans, separate refrigerated items from shelved ones; sort Dad's nails; separate Mother's buttons or spools of thread; arrange shoes from large to small or by family member; separate baby's socks from an older sibling's and Dad's; stack pans by size; set the table properly; assist in a baking project. Many events occur periodically or daily that make good learning experiences for young children because they are tasks familiar to the child. He isn't learning some remote thing he will never use. He is learning how to function in his here-and-now *and* his then-and-there world.

If you feel your child isn't interested in parts, watch him as he eats when several foods are combined into one dish. Let's say you serve a delicious beef stew. Does he eat it with gusto? Chances are he puts all the pieces of meat together, all the peas in one spot, all the potatoes in another, and all the carrots in still another. He may eat all that is on his plate, but he prefers his parts separated. Why does he behave so? Perhaps his taste buds are sensitive and he likes to have his flavors unmixed. Perhaps he hasn't developed a liking for food combinations. Or maybe he is still adhering to his early eating habits. Undoubtedly he was fed one food at a time until he consumed it.

All of the previous themes in this book can be discussed under the subject of classification. For example, a child learns there are many parts to his body; but when they are combined, they represent all of him. Each person is an individual but also a part of a family; many individual people combine to make a community function; and on and on.

The child who understands that his world is organized in smaller and larger parts is on his way to greater learning and creative freedom because he has the ability to see relationships. As a result, he will be self-confident and have the ability to solve problems as they arise.

APPENDIX: ADDITIONAL AIDS

INTRODUCTION

The information provided in this section consists of additional materials and ideas which can help you modify or enhance the themes and lesson plans included in each of the preceding chapters. Or you might even create a lesson plan of your own. The information is organized and presented in the same manner as that in each chapter, and at various points page references are provided to guide you quickly to specific information listed in a particular theme and/or lesson plan.

Chapter 2

Theme 1: I'm Important (pp. 21-27)

Concepts

- We call a person by his name so that he will know we are talking to him.
- Each person has something he likes to do or can do well.
- If a person likes himself, then he can like others, too.
- As we grow older, we can do more and different things.
- Some things you like to do by yourself, and some things you like to do with others. Doing things with others is fun.
- When people work together, they can usually do things easier and faster.
- You feel good when you do something well.

Learning Activities

- During freeplay, various materials are provided to encourage the children to work together.
- Mirrors are available, and the children are encouraged to use them and talk about what they see.
- Throughout the day, experiences are provided in which children can experiment (blocks, manipulative area, science table) and can also be and feel helpful (food experience, clean-up, various games, snack and lunch-time helps).
- Prestory activities, stories, and music will emphasize self-image and focus on the individual child.
- Especially during the outside period, the children will be encouraged to think of new ways to arrange equipment and try new large muscle activities.

Schedule of Activities

Setting the learning stage

- Talk about what the children could do when they were babies and what they can do now that they are older and larger.
- The teacher can tell something short and interesting about when she was a baby or a youngster like her preschoolers.
- Ask the children to tell what they need help with (holding a board while it is being sawed, teeter-tottering), and get them thinking about cooperating with others.

157

Prestory activities

- Poetry

  - Dwyer, Jane R. *I See a Poem.* Racine, Wisc.: Whitman Publishing Co., 1968.

    "It Was" by Dorothy Aldis, p. 26

  - Frank, J. (ed.) *Poems to Read to the Very Young.* New York: Random House, 1961.

    "Five Years Old" by Mary Louise Allen
    "Hide and Seek" by A. B. Shiffrin
    "My Dog" by Marchette Chute
    "Jump or Jiggle" by Evelyn Beyer
    "High-Heeled Shoes" by Kate Cox Goddard
    "Hiding" by Dorothy Aldis
    "Before the Bath" by Corinna Marsh
    "After A Bath" by Aileen Fisher
    "Bedtime" by Eleanor Farjean

  - Frank J. (ed.) *More Poems to Read to the Very Young.* New York: Random House, 1968.

    "Growing Up" —unknown
    "Singing Time" by Rose Fyleman
    "Dressing" by Romney Gay
    "Reflection" by Myra Cohn Livingston
    "Solution" by Leland R. Jacobs
    "Chums" by Arthur Guiterman
    "Bedtime" by Kate Cox Goddard
    "Wooley Blanket" by Kate Cox Goddard

  - Goddard, Kate Cox. *Poems for Little Ears.* New York: Platt & Munk, 1962.

    "Worries," p. 6
    "Look at Me," p. 17
    "The Looking Glass Child," p. 34
    "Pretending," p. 43
    "Growing Up," p. 58

  - Stevenson, Robert Louis. *A Child's Garden of Verses.* New York: Simon and Schuster, 1957.

    "My Shadow"

- Games

  - Have all the children with a certain similar characteristic (brown eyes, red shoes, green clothing) participate at one time.

  - Make up a story with the children, giving each child a chance to add something and then thanking him for his contribution. Use the names of the children.

Story time

- Ets, Marie Hall. *Play•With Me.* New York: Viking Press, 1955.
- Write an original story to fit the needs and interests of your children. (See Suggested Original Story, pages 159-160.)

Music

- Songs

  - Barlow, Betty M. *Do It Yourself Songs.* Delaware Water Gap, Pa.: Shawnee Press, 1969.

    "What Did Susie Wear?" p. 59

  - Berg, R. C., et al. *Music for Young Americans: Sharing Music.* New York: American Book Co., 1966.

    "New Clothes," p. 6
    "Helping Mother," p. 21

  - Jaye, M. T., and Imogene Hilyard. *Making Music Your Own.* Morristown, N. J.: Silver Burdett Co., 1966.

    "Getting Acquainted," p. 24
    "Love Somebody," p. 126

  - Mursell, J. L., et al. *Music for Living through the Day.* Morristown, N. J.: Silver Burdett Co., 1962.

    "Who Are You?" p. 3

  - Pitts, L. B., et al. *The Kindergarten Book.* Boston: Ginn and Co., 1959.

    "A Song About Me," p. 3
    "Would You Like to Know?" p. 4
    "Who Are You?" p. 5

  - Renstrom, Moiselle. *Merrily We Sing.* Salt Lake City: Pioneer Music Press, 1957.

    "Boys and Dogs," p. 17
    "Give Me Your Right Hand," p. 20
    "Many Things Make Me," p. 23
    "Monkey Talk," p. 28
    "Which Would You Rather Be?" p. 48

  - Roebeck, Lois. *Who Am I?* Chicago: Follett Publishing Co.

    "I'm a Person," p. 9

  - Smith, R., and C. Leonhard. *Discovering Music Together: Early Childhood.* Chicago: Follett Publishing Co., 1968.

158

"Pretty Mary," p. 18
"I See A Gal," p. 19
"Who's That?" p. 28

- Wood, L. F., and L. B. Scott. *Singing Fun*. St. Louis: Webster Publishing Co., 1954.

  "My Bugle," p. 52
  "How Old Are You?" p. 61

- Zeitlin, Patty. *Castle in My City*. San Carlos, Calif.: Golden Gate Junior Books, 1968.

  "I Have a Little House," p. 24
  "I Found a Little Dog," p. 40

- Records

  - Children's Record Guild

    "Do This, Do That" —#1040
    "Me, Myself, and I" —#1007
    "Nothing To Do" —#1012

  - Kimbo Educational Records, P. O. Box 246, Deal, New Jersey 07723.

    "My Name Is _____ " —(LP 7020)
    "I'm Getting Big Now" —(LP 7021)
    "What Is Your Name" —ARLP-514
    "What Are You Wearing" —ARLP-514

  - Young People's Records

    "Everyday We Grow-I-O" —#8001
    "I'm Dressing Myself" —#803

Books Available Throughout the Day

- Alexander, Anne. *I Want to Whistle*. New York: Abelard-Schuman, 1958.
- Berman, Rhoda. *When You Were a Little Baby*. New York: Lothrop, Lee and Shepard, 1954.
- Bond, Gladys B. *Patrick Will Grow*. Racine, Wis.: Whitman Publishing Co., 1966.
- Brown, Myra B. *First Night Away from Home*. New York: Franklin Watts, 1960.
- Brown, Myra B. *Benjy's Blanket*. New York: Franklin Watts, 1962.
- Bryant, Bernice. *Let's Be Friends*. Chicago: Children's Press, 1954.
- Burton, Virginia Lee. *Mike Mulligan and His Steam Shovel*. Boston: Houghton Mifflin, 1939.
- Cook, Bernadine. *The Little Fish That Got Away*. New York: Young Scott Books, 1956.
- Crume, Marion, *Let Me See You Try*. Glendale, Calif.: Bowmar, 1968.

- Duncan, Lois. *The Littlest One in the Family*. New York: Dodd, Mead, and Co., 1960.
- Francoise. *The Things I Like*. New York: Scribner's & Sons, 1960.
- Gay, Zhenya. *What's Your Name?* New York: Viking Press, 1955.
- Lund, Doris H. *Did You Ever?* New York: Parents' Magazine Press, 1965.
- Preston, Edna Mitchell. *The Temper Tantrum Book*. New York: Viking Press, 1969.
- Rice, Inez. *A Long, Long Time*. New York: Lothrop, Lee and Shepard, 1964.
- Steiner, Charlotte. *What Do You Love?* New York: Alfred A. Knopf.
- Taylor, Barbara J. *I Can Do*. Provo, Utah: Brigham Young University Press, 1972.
- Udry, Janice May. *Let's Be Enemies*. New York: Harper & Bros., 1961.
- Widerberg, Siv. *My Best Friend*. Great Britain, 1969.
- Young, W. Edward. *Norman and the Nursery School*. New York: Platt & Munk Co.
- Zion, Gene. *Dear Garbage Man*. New York: Harper & Bros.
- Zolotow, Charlotte. *If It Weren't for You*. New York: Harper and Row, 1966.

Suggested Original Story

"Meet the Different Faces of Alvin"

This story was originated by a creative student in one of my classes. However, I have not been able to locate the author to obtain her permission to print the story; therefore, only some of the basic ideas are related here.

The central character is a boy named Alvin. When he feels different moods, he "puts on different faces." The faces depicting eight different emotions are related to color ("When Alvin is mad, he puts on his red face."), but the children are more interested in Alvin's reactions than they are in the color of his face. Alvin's eight faces are made out of colored construction paper mounted on large sheets of poster paper. Each one has one or two sentences describing Alvin and his emotions. Because the children experience these same feelings in their own lives, they are very interested in Alvin's reactions.

After having looked into children's faces as they hear about Alvin, and after having seen their expressions change to match Alvin's, I have introduced the idea of using a large hand mirror. First the story of Alvin is told rather slowly so the children can see the pictures and empathize with him. Then, the second time the pictures are shown, I say something like "Let me see you when you feel *(mad, happy, sad, naughty)*." Each child has a chance to look at himself expressing the different moods.

The involvement and response of the children is exciting.

Further Topics

- Things I Can Do with My Body.
- I Do Things That Make Me Happy.
- I've Learned to Do Many Things (tie my shoes, ride a two-wheeled bike, set the table, feed my pet).
- When I Grow Up.
- I Want to Be. . . .

Chapter 2

Theme 2: My Body Works for Me (pp. 27-35)

Concepts

- There are many parts of the body.
- Each part of the body has a name.
- Different parts of the body have different uses.
- Even though each person has the same body parts, he may grow differently from someone else (be taller or heavier, have different coloring).
- The hard parts in the body are bones.
- The body is covered with a soft tissue called skin.
- The different parts of the body can be moved because of joints and muscles.

Learning Activities

- The bulletin board (on the children's eye level) will contain pictures of people involved in different physical activities. Some of the pictures will have important parts of the body missing.
- Show a skeleton.
- Use songs, games, poetry, and fingerplays emphasizing the body.
- A creative experience will help the children view their bodies as a total unit.
- A guest will visit the preschool group to help the children understand about their bodies and especially about their bones.
- Throughout the day, experiences will be provided where the children will be using their large and small muscles as well as the various parts of their bodies.

Schedule of Activities

Setting the learning stage

- Review preassessment.
- Use visual aids and conversation relating to the body (see Suggested Verbalization or Ideas on page 162).
- Display a skeleton and talk about the different bones and parts of the body.

Free play

- Creative materials: provide old magazines from which the children can cut pictures of people or parts of the body. Include paper and paste.
- Sensory table: supply it with water and some boats.

Prestory activities

- Fingerplays
  - Grayson, Marion. *Let's Do Fingerplays.* Washington: Robert B. Luce, 1962.

    "This Is the Circle That Is My Head," p. 14
    "Dressing," p. 16
    "Hands on Shoulders," p. 13
    "Five Fingers," p. 11
    "Clap Your Hands," p. 10
    "Jack-in-the-Box," p. 55
    "Who Feels Happy?" p. 76

- Poetry
  - Aldis, Dorothy. *Everything & Anything.* New York: Minton, Balch, 1927.

    "A Thought," p. 59
    "Mouths," p. 87

  - Govoni, Ilse Hayes and Dorothy Hall Smith (ed.). *The Golden Picture Book of Poems.* New York: Simon and Schuster, 1955.

    "Jump or Jiggle" by Evelyn Beyer, p. 46
    "Everybody Says" by Dorothy Aldis, p. 4
    "Drinking Fountain" by Marchette Chute, p. 20

  - Stevenson, Robert Louis. *A Child's Garden of Verses.* Philadelphia: David McKay Co., 1916.

    "My Shadow"

- Games
  - Show a picture of someone engaged in a physical activity and ask the children what parts of the body the person is using.

- Describe someone in action and see if the children can guess what the person is doing (he throws and catches a ball, wears a mitt on his hand, and swings a bat).
- Ask the children to demonstrate different activities they can perform.
- Describe a part of the body and see if the children can guess what part it is.
- Ask the children what they can do with different parts of the body. Name as many uses as possible.

Story time (Guest)

Instead of having a regular story time this day, invite a guest to help you—perhaps a doctor. Be sure to tell him what your theme is, what ages the children are, and specifically how you would like him to enforce your concepts.

One doctor who visited a group of preschool children explained and demonstrated how he took care of broken bones. He showed the children the materials he used and how he set broken bones, and to make the experience more meaningful, he asked if any child would like to pretend he had a broken arm so the doctor could show how he would fix it. Strangely enough (it was too real to the children) he got no volunteers, so he asked the teacher. He put a soft piece of cloth on the teacher's arm. Then he soaked a roll of gauze material in some water. When it was softened, he rolled it around the teacher's arm, and in a few minutes, it hardened into a cast. The children looked at the cast, felt it, and asked questions about it. Then the doctor explained how he would remove the cast when the bone had mended. He removed it, and, even though the children were unsure about the removal, they all stayed to watch and ask questions. They enjoyed looking at, feeling, and talking about the cast and the broken arm.

Music

- Songs
  - Choate, R. A., et al. *Music for Early Childhood.* New York: American Book Co., 1970.

    "Hokey Pokey," p. 10
  - Pitts, L. B., et al. *The Kindergarten Book.* Boston: Ginn and Co., 1959.

    "A Song About Me," p. 3
    See "Singing While We Play," pp. 8-33.

- Renstrom, Moiselle. *Merrily We Sing.* Salt Lake City: Pioneer Music Press, 1962.

  "Many Things Make Me," p. 23
- Seeger, Ruth. *American Folk Songs for Children.* Garden City, N.Y.: Doubleday, 1948.

  "What Shall We Do When We All Go Out?" p. 59
  "Jim Along Josie," pp. 72-75
  "Clap Your Hands," pp. 86-87
- Wood, L. F., and L. B. Scott. *Singing Fun.* St. Louis: Webster Publishing Co., 1954.

  "I Wiggle," p. 56
  "Jack-in-the-Box," p. 57
  "My Hands," p. 58
  "Two Little Hands," p. 59
- Wood, L. F. and L. B. Scott. *More Singing Fun.* St. Louis: Webster Division, McGraw-Hill Book Co., 1961.

  "Touch Your Head," p. 69

- Records
  - Children's Record Guild

    "When I Was Very Young," #1031
  - Children's Music Center, 5373 West Pico Boulevard, Los Angeles, Calif. 90019

    "Do You Know How You Grow? Inside" (#C734)
    "Do You Know How You Grow? Outside" (#C735)

Suggested Learning Card

(School or teacher's name)	(Date)

Theme: My Body

Today we talked about our bodies. We learned that there are many important parts to our bodies and that different parts of our bodies have different names.
We saw a skeleton of a body, did finger plays, and sang songs about our bodies.
A doctor showed us how he puts a cast on a broken arm and how he removes it.
We learned that different parts of our bodies work together so we can do many things.

Suggested Verbalization or Ideas

(This is too much information for one day. Use only general ideas or dwell on a specific aspect for one day.)

It takes my whole body working together so I can do different things. One part of it needs the help of all the other parts.

The hard parts in my body are bones. Bones are hard on the outside and hollow in the center. We cannot see our bones because they are covered with flesh and skin. If you look at a skeleton, you can see the different bones.

My whole body is covered with a soft tissue called skin which is thin and tight although it may be elastic. That means it can stretch. When a person gets fat, his skin stretches to cover his body. As I grow, my skin stretches to cover my body.

Look at my hands. I have four fingers and one thumb on each hand. My thumb is on the side of my hand. When I press my thumb against my fingers, I can hold or pick up objects. I learned to do this when I was a baby. This is called the pincer grasp.

I like to feel things with my hands because it helps me learn about the objects. This is called the sense of touch. I like to touch a warm pony, soft flowers, damp sand, or a slick boat. But most of all I like to touch my cuddly teddy bear and warm blanket. What do you like to touch?

I can bend my fingers and thumbs because I have joints and muscles. A joint is a place where two bones are connected, usually so that they can move. A muscle lets me move and connects the finger to the rest of my hand. Joints (knuckles) in my hand at the base of my fingers make it easier for me to use my fingers.

At the upper part of the end joint of each finger, I have a hard substance called a fingernail. At the base of the fingernail is the cuticle. At the very tip of my finger is a part of my fingernail which is not attached to my finger and sometimes this part gets broken. I can't feel it when my fingernails are trimmed like I can when my finger gets cut. Once I shut my finger in a door and my fingernail turned black and blue.

The back of my hand sometimes gets rough and sore because of the cold or dry weather. The inside of my hand is smooth and soft and is called the palm. When I put my fingers into the palm of my hand and hold them with my thumb, I am clenching my fist.

I can do fingerplays with my fingers. I can also fingerpaint or make hand prints. I can put gloves or rings on my fingers.

162

Further Topics

- My Hands and Arms Are Useful.
- About My Feet and Legs.
- About My Senses (each one would be a separate unit).
- About My Eyes (also ears, nose, mouth).
- About My Heart (also other internal organs).
- About My Muscles (also bones, nerves, etc.).
- I Can Do Many Things with My Body.

Chapter 2

Theme 3: My Hands and Arms are Useful (pp. 35-40)

Learning Activities

- Provide manipulative toys during free play (peg boards, puzzles, balls, tinker toys.
- Have verbal discussions during the snack, free play, story time, music time, outside play. (See Suggested Verbalization or Ideas in the left-hand column.)
- Do musical activities using rhythm instruments.
- Use appropriate stories.
- Provide outside experiences which require the children to use their hands and arms.

Schedule of Activities

Setting the learning stage

- Describe how hands and arms are part of the body.
- Introduce the "feel" box. (Children can identify the objects from a box or sack by feel rather than by sight.)
- Show pictures of animals. Ask the children what they can do with their hands that animals can't do because they don't have hands.

Free play

- Blocks: place in large hollow ones cars and replicas of animals and people.
- Creative expression: prepare the easel. Provide for woodworking.
- Sensory table: different materials can be used different days (rice, sawdust, wheat, cornmeal, flour, water).

Prestory activities

- Finger plays
  - Grayson, Marion. *Let's Do Fingerplays.* Washington: Robert B. Luce, 1962.

"Open, Close Them," p. 79
"Two Little Hands," p. 12
"Five Little Indians," p. 61
"Johnny's Hammer," p. 67
"This Old Man," p. 68
"Five Little Girls," p. 20
"Sleepy Fingers," p. 43
"Playmates," p. 54
"Thumbkin Says 'I'll Dance,' " p. 8
"Where Is Thumbkin?" pp. 6-7
"My Hands," p. 12
"Busy Fingers," p. 3
"Ten Fingers," p. 3
"I Am a Fine Musician," p. 78

- Jacobs, Frances E. *Finger Plays and Action Rhymes.* New York: Lothrop, Lee and Shepard, 1968.

  "Counting the Fingers," p. 3

- McGuire, Mabelle B. *Finger & Action Rhymes.* Dansville, N.Y.: Instructor Publishing, 1966.

  "Finger Vocabulary," p. 17
  "My Hands Are Grand," p. 18
  "Popcorn," p. 19

- Poetry
  - Aldis, Dorothy. *Everything and Anything.* New York: Minton, Balch & Co., 1927.

    "Hands," pp. 53-54

  - Goddard, Kate C. *Poems for Little Ears.* New York: Platt & Munk, 1962.

    "Sticky Fingers," p. 37

  - Govoni, H., and D. H. Smith (ed.). *The Golden Picture Book of Poems.* New York: Simon & Schuster, 1955.

    "Holding Hands" by Lenore M. Link, p. 26

  - O'Neill, Mary. *Fingers Are Always Bringing Me News.* Garden City, N.Y.: Doubleday and Co., 1969.

    Many appropriate poems.

Story time

As a diversion from the theme, plan several stories which will be of particular interest to your group. You may use only one story, but if you plan for more, you will be ready in case they are needed. Here are a few suggestions:

- Freeman, Don. *Mop Top.* Chicago: Children's Press, 1955.
- Moore, Lilian. *Too Many Bozos.* New York: Golden Press, 1969.
- Keats, Ezra. *Peter's Chair.* New York: Harper & Row.

Music

- Songs
  - Berg, R. C. *Music for Young Americans: Sharing Music.* New York: American Book Co., 1966.

    "The Wiggle Song," p. 56
    "Fingers, Nose, and Toes," p. 58

  - Choate, R. A., et al. *Music for Early Childhood.* New York: American Book Co., 1970.

    "Things I Touch "

  - Jaye, M. T., and Imogene Hilyard. *Making Music Your Own.* Morristown, N.J.: Silver Burdett Co., 1966.

    "Open, Shut Them," p. 14
    "Let's Go Walking," p. 27

  - Pitts, L. B., et al. *The Kindergarten Book.* Boston: Ginn and Co., 1959.

    "Clapping Game," p. 49
    "Clapping and Stamping," p. 10
    "This Is the Way We Wash Our Hands," p. 100
    "Hop Up, Hop Down," p. 21

  - Smith, R., and C. Leonhard. *Discovering Music Together: Early Childhood.* Chicago: Follett Publishing Co., 1968.

    "Clap Your Hands," p. 39

- Record
  - "A Visit to My Little Friend," Children's Record Guild—#CRG 1017

Suggested Verbalization or Ideas

Much more can be added to the following to include all parts of the body; however, children have a more valuable time with a few specifics that they can repeat over and over and, as a result, understand at the time.

Of my whole body, hands and arms are just a part.
But when I want to do something, they help me start.

Have you ever wondered what I can do?
Just ask me, and I will show you.

Each one of my fingers has its own special name,
And I use them all when I play a game.
There's pointer, middle man, ring finger, and baby,
I might use them together—or singly, maybe.

Pointer finger stood tall one day
And waited for middle man to come to play.
Ring finger came along to call;
Baby finger was the last of all.
Thumb jumped out from the side of the hand
And said, "I want to join this merry band."

My fingers help me learn to count.
From one to ten is quite an amount.

Besides working finger plays, pegboards, and toys,
My finger goes to my lips to stop all the noise.

My hands and fingers can do creative things
And a lot of happiness bring.
I can paint, draw, cut, or paste.
Even my shoe with my hands can be laced.

There are objects I can thread on yarn or on strings,
Like cereal, beads, paper, macaroni, and other things.

I like to fingerpaint with something smooth and cool
Or splash my hands in water in a pool.

It is fun to make a puzzle or turn pages in a book,
While someone reads me a story—or I just look.

More ideas are included in "Especially for Parents" (pp. 50-52).

Further Topics:
- The Sense of Touch.
- More about Hands and Arms (clock, chair, machines).

Chapter 2

Theme 4: It's My Birthday (pp. 40-46)

Schedule of Activities

Setting the learning stage
- Ask the children how many fun or nice things they can do for (a) a parent's birthday, (b) a friend's birthday, (c) a brother's or a sister's birthday, (d) their own birthday.
- Talk about sharing your birthday with others.

- Show pictures of children at a birthday party and stimulate the children to talk about the pictures and parties.
- Tell about a birthday that was special to you when you were a child.

Free play
- Food experience: make and decorate cookies or cupcakes. (Making ice cream is often adult-centered and/or too time consuming for young hands and arms.)
- Creative expression: make simple party favors: marshmallows, gum drops, colored toothpicks, and so on.
- Sensory or Science table: today use wheat with measuring cups and funnels with large holes.

Story time
- Make up an original story about birthdays that will teach the desired concepts and be especially interesting to your children.
- See Suggested Original Stories (p. 165) for some additional ideas.

Music
- Songs
  - Jaye, M. T., and Imogene Hilyard. *Making Music Your Own.* Morristown, N.J.: Silver Burdett Co., 1966.

    "Happy Birthday," p. 3
    Also poem "Five Years Old" by Marie Louise Allen, p. 3

  - McLaughlin, R., and Lucille Wood. *The Small Singer.* Glendale, Calif.: Bowmar, 1969.

    "Birthday Song," p. 56

  - Pitts, L. B., et al. *The Kindergarten Book.* Boston: Ginn & Co., 1959.

    "My Birthday Is Today," p. 71
    "Happy Birthday," p. 72

  - Smith, R., and C. Leonhard. *Discovering Music Together: Early Childhood.* Chicago: Follett Publishing Co., 1968.

    "Rosa's Having a Birthday," p. 175

  - Wolfe, I., et al. *Music Round the Clock.* Chicago: Follett Publishing Co., 1959.

    "Happy Birthday," p. 72

Suggested Original Stories

It's an Unbirthday Day

Chances are you will have several children who do not have birthdays during the regular school year. They may feel slighted because of this, so have a special day and let them help with the plans. Originate a story about an *unbirthday* or have the children help make up one about the things they'd like to do on their birthdays. You might even include a teacher's birthday in the story just to let the children know that teachers also have birthdays.

I Want to Change My Birthday

Make up a story about a child who always wanted to change his birthday (because it was too close to Christmas, because he thought it would be more fun to have a party in the winter than in the summer, because he wanted to have it the same time as a friend, because he wanted to have it when no one else was having one). After weighing all the different possibilities, he finally decides that the date of his real birthday is the best time of all.

Further Topics

● Different Holidays.
● We Had an "Unbirthday".
● Special Events (family, community, and church).

Chapter 3

Theme 1: We're a Family (pp. 57-62)

Schedule of Activities

Setting the learning stage

Have a family member come and visit with the children (a grandparent would be especially nice). Have the member stay throughout the morning and interact with the children. For example, a grandmother could help make cookies, a grandfather could demonstrate woodworking, or a brother or sister could share a pet or hobby.

Free play

● Housekeeping area: add dress-up clothes for both boys and girls.

● Blocks: use large hollow blocks or a wooden structure which is covered with a sheet or blanket to give a homey feeling.

Story time

Instead of having a formal story time, have one of your guests tell some of the fun things he has done with his family. The guest might even bring some props (something of interest to the children, such as pictures, a scrapbook, or an item he and his family have made).

Books Available Throughout the Day

● Berman, Rhoda. *When You Were a Little Baby*. New York: Lothrop, Lee and Shepard.
● Duvoisin, Roger. *The House of Four Seasons*. New York: Lothrop, Lee and Shepard.
● Lenski, Lois. *Papa Small*. New York: Henry Z. Walck, 1951.
● McRoberts, Agnesann. *Two New Babies*. Racine, Wis.: Whitman Publishing Co.
● Radlauer, Ruth and Ed. *Father Is Big*. Glendale, Calif.: Bowmar, 1967.
● Simon, Norma. *The Daddy Days*. New York: Abelard-Schuman, 1958.
● Steiner, Charlotte. *Daddy Comes Home*. Garden City, N.Y.: Doubleday and Co., 1944.
● Watts, Mabel. *My Father Can Fix Anything*. Racine, Wis.: Whitman Publishing Co., 1965.
● Zolotow, Charlotte. *Big Brother*. New York: Harper.

Music
● Songs

   ● Dalton, Arlene, et al. *My Picture Book of Songs*. Chicago: M.A. Donohue & Co., 1947.

      "My Grandma," p. 25
      "Helping Mother," p. 25

   ● Mursell, James L., et al. *Music for Living through the Day*. Chicago: Silver Burdett Co., Teacher's Book One, 1962.

      Section on "Home Sweet Home," pp. 25-46.

   ● Wood, Lucille F., and L. B. Scott. *Singing Fun*. St. Louis: Webster Div., McGraw-Hill Book Co., 1954.

      Section on "My Family and My Town," pp. 47-54.

Further Topics

- Spend a day focusing on each family member (your immediate family).
- Introduce cousins, uncles and aunts, grandparents (your extended family).
- Talk about people who may live with us though they are not related.
- Talk about different kinds of houses people live in (teepee, igloo, boat).

Chapter 3

Theme 2: Friends Are Fun (pp. 62-67)

Schedule of Activities

Music

- Records
    - "A Visit to My Little Friend," Children's Record Guild #1017
    - "My Playmate the Wind," Young People's Record #4501
- Songs
    - Mursell, J. L., et al. *Music for Living through the Day.* Chicago: Silver Burdett, 1962.

        Section on "Getting Acquainted," pp. 1-25

    - Pitts, L. B., et al. *The Kindergarten Book.* Boston: Ginn and Co., 1959.

        Many appropriate selections.

Story time

Read to the children a story about a child who goes to nursery school and meets friends of different races and backgrounds. The child describes each child and tells something special he likes about each one.

Further Topics

- My Friends and I.
- Let's Cooperate.
- Let's Share.
- I Do Things That Make Others Happy.
- Others Do Things That Make Me Happy.

Chapter 3

Theme 3: Many People Live in My Community (pp. 67-72)

Preassessment

- Select some helpers who are important to your community (dentist, barber, mechanic, farmer) and ask questions which will help you find out what the children already know about them. Plan appropriate means of giving accurate information to the children. Watch the interests of the children. If they are really interested, continue with helpers. If they become bored, shift to another theme and come back to this one later, if appropriate.

Concepts

- Have well in mind what concepts are important for dealing with each helper, such as where he works, what he wears when he works, what he is called.
- Emphasize the value of people working together.

Learning Activities

- Field trips are necessary in order for the experiences to be most valuable. Plan them carefully so as not to bombard the children. Invite many helpers to your center (this reduces the fatigue of the children and the amount of time and risk involved).

Schedule of Activities

Music

- Songs
    - Dalton, Arlene, et al. *My Picture Book of Songs.* Chicago: M.A. Donohue & Co., 1947.

        "The Postman," p. 41

    - McLaughlin, Robert, and Lucille Wood. *The Small Singer.* Glendale, Calif.: Bowmar, 1969.

        "The Fire Truck"

    - Mursell, J. L. *Music for Living through the Day.* Chicago: Silver Burdett Co., 1962. Teacher's Book One.

        Section 5, "I Like the City," pp. 87-108

    - Pitts, L. B., et al. *The Kindergarten Book.* New York: Ginn and Co., 1959.

        Many appropriate selections.

Further Topics

- Ways Different People Help Me (neighbors, friends, community people).

● More depth about individual occupations.

Chapter 3

Theme 4: The Policeman Helps Me (pp. 72-78)

Schedule of Activities

Free play

● Now that the policeman has come to your school where the surroundings are somewhat friendly or familiar to the children, you could next visit a police station or jail.
● With blocks or large boxes, make cars (large enough for the children to climb in and out).

Prestory Activities

● Puppets: use puppets to portray a variety of community helpers and have them interact, telling each other what they do in the community or how they work together. Involve the children with the puppets and dialogue and assess their knowledge.
● Poetry: Govoni, H., and D. H. Smith. *The Golden Picture Book of Poems.* New York: Simon and Schuster, 1955.

  ● "The Policeman" by Marjorie S. Watts, p. 17

Music

● Songs
  ● Berg, R. C., et al. *Music for Young Americans: Sharing Music.* New York: American Book Co., 1966.

    "The Traffic Policeman," p. 23
  ● Choate, R. A., et al. *Music for Early Childhood.* New York: American Book Co., 1970.

    "I Like the Policeman," p. 96
  ● Jaye, M. T., and Imogene Hilyard. *Making Music Your Own.* Morristown, N. J.: Silver Burdett Co., 1966.

    "Mister Policeman," p. 9
  ● McLaughlin, R., and Lucille Wood. Sing a Song. Glendale, Calif.: Bowmar, 1969.

    "The Policeman," p. 25
  ● Wolfe, I., et al. *Music Round about Us.* Chicago: Follett Publishing Co.

    "The Policeman's Song," p. 23
  ● Wood & Scott. *Singing Fun.* St. Louis: Webster Publishing Co., 1943.

    "Policeman," p. 50

Outside activities

● Time and equipment for large muscle use should be provided even when the activities are not geared to the theme of the day.
● Try a new obstacle course.
● Provide appropriate props—white gloves, whistles.
● Bring a walkie-talkie and let the children use it.

Further Topics

● Different Kinds of Policemen (harbor patrol, mounted police, highway patrol, canine corps).
● Different Uniforms.
● Laws and Rules (privileges and responsibilities at home, school, church, community).
● Safety.

Chapter 4

Theme 1: Farm Animals Interest Me (pp. 87-93)

Schedule of Activities

Free play

● After introducing the subject to the children, use this plan as preassessment for a trip to a local farm.
● Let the children make sack puppets that resemble animals.

Prestory activity or story time

● Use a short film about animals or a trip to a farm such as:

"The Cow," CFP 1968, 10 minutes, color Rental $4.50
"Pigs," CFP 1967, 11 minutes, color   Rental $4.50

  These are produced by Churchill Films and can be ordered from Brigham Young University, Educational Media Services, Herald R. Clark Building, Provo, Utah 84602. Both of these films have musical backgrounds but no narration. Children can therefore ask questions and teachers can point out things as the film progresses.
● Have a tape recorder with a tape of animal sounds. Let the children hear the sounds and then try to

imitate them. Record the children's sounds and then play back both sets of sounds.

Music

- Songs

  - Dalton, Arlene, et al. *My Picture Book of Songs.* Chicago: M. A. Donohue and Co., 1947.

    "Grandpa's Farm," p. 57

  - Pitts, L. B., et al. *The Kindergarten Book.* Boston: Ginn and Co., 1959.

    Section "About Farm Animals," pp. 114-118

Books Available Throughout the Day

- Crume, Marion W. *Furry Boy.* Glendale, Calif.: Bowmar, 1969.
- Crume, Marion W. *I Like Cats.* Glendale, Calif.: Bowmar, 1968.
- Cook, Bernadine. *The Curious Little Kitten.* New York: Young Scott, 1956.
- Hall, Bill. *What Ever Happens to Puppies?* New York: Golden Press, 1965.
- Moore, Lillian. *Too Many Bozos.* New York: Golden Press.
- Nodset, Joan. *Go Away, Dog.* New York: Harper and Row, 1965.
- Zion, Gene. *Harry the Dirty Dog.* New York: Harper, 1956.
- _____. *No Roses for Harry.* New York: Harper, 1958.

Further Topics

- A day or unit on pets.
- Zoo or wild animals.
- Birds.
- Insects.
- Reptiles.

Chapter 4

Theme 2: Plants Provide Things for Me (pp. 93-99)

Schedule of Activities

- If other better aids are not available, you can use the pictures on seed packets to show the children or have them use these to cut and paste.
- Place a plant in your room and an identical one in a dark room. Water one plant, but not the other and

make periodic comparisons between the plants with the children.

- Obtain small pots or use cut-down milk cartons and plant bulbs (instead of ordinary seeds) in them for the children to take home.
- Use a magnifying glass to look at different roots, leaves, stems, flowers.

Further Topics

- Go into further detail about the edible parts of plants.
- Discuss plants which are harmful when eaten, plants which are used for beauty instead of for food.
- Talk about the different kinds of coverings on fruits and vegetables (for instance, how some are edible and some are not, how easily they are removed).
- Talk about foods of the same color.
- Discuss nutrition and perhaps introduce the basic four food groups.
- Spend a day or unit on trees and their uses.
- Devote a day to flowers.
- Talk about where plants grow (for example, under water, in the desert, on rocks).
- Discuss preparation of different foods (raw or cooked).
- Talk about food eaten by pets and other animals.

Chapter 4

Theme 3: I Love Water (pp. 99-106)

Schedule of Activities

Setting the learning stage

- Talk about weather and water. Show pictures (of frost on windows, snow on trees, sprinkler on lawn, boats on lake).
- Ask the children to name what season it is now and how water is present. Use pictures. Talk about another season and how water is evident then.
- Show some pictures and describe some sport or recreation using water. How do we use the water differently for each (skiing, ice skating, swimming, boating)?
- Show wearing apparel and talk about what kind of water activity it is used for. Using a tub or pan show and discuss the different materials used for water activities (fast-drying materials for swimsuits, rubber boots for rainy weather, water-repellent materials for

snowsuits and outer wear, plastics for raincoats and umbrellas, aprons or smocks for painting). Introduce words such as *absorbent, evaporation, repellent.*

Free play

- Housekeeping area: dolls can be bathed. Provide towels and doll clothes.
- Food experience: add hot water to gelatin and cool in the refrigerator for the snack. Have a vegetable or fruit press and squeeze fruit to make juice (indicates that water is present). Or make and freeze popsicles. Make soup.
- Creative materials: in a water table, have boats. Let the children help make finger paint with soap flakes, water, and egg beaters.
- Science or sensory table: provide tubs of water and various items for the children to watch float or sink. Introduce the word *buoyancy* and demonstrate its meaning. Have plants and a watering can for watering them. Empty and clean a fishbowl or aquarium. Provide a tub of water, canvas shoes, leather shoes, rubber boots, and rubber shoes (thongs). Let the children see how the shoes absorb water. Then put dry shoes inside the boots and observe that they stay dry. Discuss why they stay dry and why we wear boots.

Prestory activities

- Poetry
  - Aldis, Dorothy. *Everything and Anything.* New York: Minton, Balch, 1927.

    "The Sprinkler," p. 93
    "A Good Thing," p. 39
    "The Rain," p. 67

  - Dwyer, Jane E. *I See a Poem.* Racine, Wisconsin: Whitman Publishing Co., 1968.

    "Mud" by Polly Chase Boyden, p. 14
    "When It Rains" by Aileen Fisher, p. 14
    "Spring Rain" by Marchette Chute, p. 15
    "Come on In," p. 21

  - Field, Rachel. *Taxis and Toadstools.* New York: Doubleday, 1926.

    "City Rain"

  - Govoni, I. H., and D. H. Smith (ed.). *The Golden Picture Book of Poems.* New York: Simon and Schuster, 1955.

    "Water Noises," p. 13

    "Drinking Fountain," p. 20
    "Rain," p. 30
    "Spring Rain," p. 31

  - Milne, A. A. *When We Were Very Young.* New York: E. P. Dutton and Co., 1952.

    "Happiness," p. 4

  - Smith R., and C. Leonhard. *Discovering Music: Early Childhood.* Chicago: Follett Publishing Co., 1968.

    "Raining Again Today," by Dorothy Aldis, p. 27

  - Stevenson, Robert Louis. *A Child's Garden of Verse.* New York: Oxford Press, 1947.

    "Where Go the Boats," p. 20
    "Rain," p. 57

Music

- Songs
  - Berg, R. C., et al. *Music for Young Americans: Sharing Music.* New York: American Book Co., 1966.

    "Bumbershoot," p. 37
    "Rain," p. 38
    "Listen to the Rain," p. 38
    "Eency Weency Spider," p. 74

  - Choate, R. A., et al. *Music for Early Childhood.* New York: American Book Co., 1970.

    "Rain," p. 26
    "Rainbow Song," p. 74

  - Choate, R. A., et al. *New Dimensions in Music: Beginning Music.* New York: American Book Co., 1970.

    "City Rain," p. 63
    "Pitter Patter," p. 65

  - Dalton, Arlene, Myriel Ashton, and Erla Young. *My Picture Book of Songs.* Chicago: M. A. Donohue & Co., 1947.

    "The Motor Boat," p. 19
    "Mr. Snowman," p. 37
    "Pitter Pat," p. 53
    "Little Drippy Drops," p. 53

  - Jaye, M. T., and Imogene Hilyard. *Making Music Your Own.* Morristown, N. J.: Silver Burdett Co., 1966.

"Raindrops," p. 15
"Japanese Rain Song," p. 68
"Weather Song," p. 133

- MacCarteney, Laura P. *Songs for the Nursery School.* Cincinnati: Willis Music, 1937.

  "Little Pool," p. 52
  "It's Raining on the Town," p. 59
  "Puddles," p. 59
  " 'Tis Raining," p. 60

- McLaughlin, R., and Lucille Wood. *The Small Singer.* Glendale, Calif.: Bowmar, 1969.

  "How Many Raindrops?" p. 27
  "Raindrops," p. 29
  "It Rained a Mist," p. 30
  "Lullaby of the Rain," p. 31
  "On a Rainy Day," p. 31

- Mursell, J. L., et al. *Music for Living Now and Long Ago.* Morristown, N. J.: Silver Burdett Co., 1962. Teacher's Book Three.

  "Listen to the Rain," p. 130

- Mursell, J. L., et al. *Music for Living through the Day.* Morristown, N. J.: Silver Burdett Co., 1962.

  "I Like Rain," p. 128

- Pitts, L. B., et al. *The Kindergarten Book.* Boston: Ginn & Co., 1959.

  "Spit, Spat, Spatter," p. 97
  "Under My Umbrella," p. 98
  "Rain," p. 98

- Siebold, Meta. *Happy Songs for Happy Children.* New York: Schirmer, 1928.

  "April Showers," p. 16
  "Rubber Boots," p. 23
  "Raining," p. 24

- Smith, R., and C. Leonhard. *Discovering Music: Early Childhood.* Chicago: Follett Publishing Co., 1968.

  "Raining Again Today," p. 27

- Records

  - Children's Record Guide "Indoors When It Rains," #1021

  - Young People's Records "Rainy Day," #712

Snack or lunch

If something was not prepared earlier, you can provide frozen fruit concentrate and let the children help add the water and stir. Or you can make lemonade by squeezing the lemons and adding sugar and water.

Outside activities

If weather permits, provide a wading pool; have the hose running down the slide; use water in the sand area—make dams and canals; water plants using the hose and/or sprinkling cans; provide a tub filled with water, a bucket, and a hose, and show the children how to siphon water. Use the word *siphon* and demonstrate its meaning.

Books Available Throughout the Day

- Andrews, Martin. *Fish.* New York: Platt & Munk, 1968.
- Cook, Bernadine. *The Little Fish That Got Away.* New York: Young Scott Books, 1956.
- Darby, Gene. *What Is Water?* Chicago: Benefic Press.
- Francoise. *The Big Rain.* Charles Scribner's Sons, 1961.
- Goudey, Alice E. *The Good Rain.* New York: E. P. Dutton & Co., 1950.
- Jordan, Helen J. *Seeds by Wind and Water.* New York: Thomas Y. Crowell Co., 1954.
- Simon, Norma. *The Wet World.* New York: J. B. Lippincott Co., 1954.
- Smith, Wm. J. *It Rains—It Shines.* New York: Harvey House, 1967.
- Zion, Gene. *Really Spring.* New York: Harper & Bros., 1956.
- _____. *Harry by the Sea.* New York: Harper & Bros., 1965.

Further Topics

- Transportation on Water.
- Water Wheels and Windmills.
- Dams (Rivers, Reservoirs, Lakes).
- How Plants Get Water.
- Weather (Rain, Snow, Fog).
- Evaporation.
- Water Sports and Recreation.
- Water Everyday.
- The Day the Water Was Turned Off.
- Occupations That Depend on Water (Fishing, Shipping, Logging, Plumbing).

Further Topics Related to the Chapter in General

- Air and/or Wind.
- Soil and Erosion.
- Rocks and Crystals.
- Chemistry and Combinations of Materials.
- Sun, Moon, and Stars.
- Electricity.
- Energy Sources (Heat and Light).
- Machines.
- Liquids, Solids, and Gases.
- Sound and Vibration.
- Pollution.
- Magnets.
- Pulleys.
- Communication Systems.
- Seasons.

Chapter 5

Theme 1: Music in My Life (pp. 114-121)

Schedule of Activities

- Provide commercial rhythm instruments and let the children explore and experiment with them. Let them use them to music, **and** arrange for each child to have an opportunity to use a variety of instruments. Don't expect too much the first few times the children use instruments. Remember, the ability to keep time to music improves with maturity (Read, 1971).
- If possible, visit a local school where a band or orchestra is rehearsing and arrange for the conductor to show the different instruments to the children. A visit could be made when a marching band is practicing.
- Ask the parents of the children to assist you. Perhaps some of them play instruments and would like to share their talents with the children. Siblings who play instruments are admired by young children—and it is good for that sibling to share his talent.

Books Available Throughout the Day

- Aliki. *My Five Senses.* New York: Thomas Y. Crowell Co., 1962.
- Borton, Helen. *Do You Hear What I Hear?* New York: Abelard-Schuman, 1960.
- Brown, Margaret W. *The Summer Noisy Book.* New York: Harper and Row, 1951.
- _____ . *The Indoor Noisy Book.* New York: Harper and Row, 1942.
- _____ . *The Country Noisy Book.* New York: Harper and Row, 1940.
- _____ . *The Quiet Noisy Book.* New York: Harper and Row, 1950.
- Crume, Marion W. *Listen!* Glendale, Calif.: Bowmar, 1968.
- Garelick, Mae. *Sounds of a Summer Night.* New York: Young Scott Books.
- Podendorf, Illa. *The True Book of Sounds We Hear.* Chicago: Children's Press, 1963.
- Schulevitz, Uri. *Oh, What a Noise.* New York: Macmillan Co., 1971.

Schedule of Activities

Music

- Pitts, L. B.; et al. *The Kindergarten Book.* New York: Ginn and Co., 1959.
- Renstrom, Moiselle. *Musical Adventures.* Salt Lake City: Deseret Book, 1943.

  "Little Music Box," p. 17

Finger plays

- Jacobs, Frances E. *Finger Plays and Action Rhymes.* New York: Lothrop, Lee & Shepard, 1941.

  "Music," p. 53

Further Topics

- Individual instruments
- More depth on each *kind* of instrument
- Sound
- Vibration
- Pitch—high and low
- Rhythm

Chapter 5

Theme 2: Give Me Color (pp. 121-128)

Schedule of Activities

Setting the learning stage

- Play a color game. Show a color and if a child is wearing that same color, have him stand up. Make sure everyone has a turn.

- Sing a song emphasizing color.
- Ask the children which of them brought something from home that was a particular color. Let them show it.
- Ask the children to think about and name things in their room at home that are a particular color.

Free play

- Housekeeping area: supply attractively arranged plastic fruits and vegetables, empty food boxes, and cartons. Also provide dress-up clothes.
- Creative expression: let the children mix paint for use at the easel (primary, secondary, and/or pastels). Have pieces of colored cellophane or color paddles for the children to put together to form different colors. Provide colored objects for stringing—macaroni, yarn, paper, straws, cereal, buttons.

  Grate old crayons with a food grater. Place the colored particles between sheets of waxed paper and press the paper with a warm iron. The crayons melt and make a design sealed between the sheets. (Requires supervision.) Encourage the children to draw with crayons on a piece of butcher paper and then brush paint over the crayons. The paper will resist the paint where the crayons have been applied.

  If the children are old enough or if you have enough help you might try dyeing some fabrics or even tie-dyeing. Children could help dye macaroni, egg shells, rice, among other things, for collage or for another creative experience. Provide scissors and multicolored fabric. Let the children cut out the colors of their choice.
- Manipulative area: provide small, colored, plastic or wood objects which can be fitted together. Use boards and colored pegs.
- Science table: supply colored water, soap flakes, straws.
- Book corner and books: see books listed at end of plan.

Prestory activities

- Games
  - Put common objects in a paper sack or box and have each child pull something from the sack and name its color. (If the children are old enough, they can describe the object to the other children to see if they can guess what color it is before they see it.)
  - Give each child a paint chip, a piece of colored paper, or a piece of fabric and have him match it to one of many objects displayed on a table.
  - Have a child touch all children on the head who are wearing a certain color.
  - Ask the children to demonstrate how certain colors make them feel (may be too advanced).
  - Show pictures of various seasons and help the children identify the most common colors for each season.

Story time

Write an original story that will appeal to your children and emphasize the concepts they need. See Suggested Original Stories (p. 173). You might even want your story to be a diversion from the theme of the day, or you may have some special requests or favorites of the children that will be fun.

Music

- Songs
  - Caines, Gracia. *Happy Songs for Children*. Cincinnati: Willis Music Co., 1957.

    "Rainbow in My Garden," p. 22
  - Choate, R. A., et al. *Music for Early Childhood*. New York: American Book Co., 1970.

    "Stop! Stop! Look at the Light!" p. 113
    "Color Song," p. 127
  - Dalton, Alene, et al. *My Picture Book of Songs*. Chicago: M. A. Donohue & Co., 1947.

    "Red! White! Blue!" p. 43
  - Jaye, M. T., and Imogene Hilyard. *Making Music Your Own*. Morristown, N.J.: Silver Burdett Co., 1966.

    "What Do You Do?" p. 11
    "Mary Wore a Red Dress," p. 12
  - Mursel, et al. *Music through the Day*. Morristown, N.J.: Silver Burdett Co., 1962.

    "The Green Dress," p. 27
    "Little White Daisies," p. 3
  - Smith, R., and C. Leonhard. *Discovering Music Together: Early Childhood*. Chicago: Follett Publishing Co., 1968.

    "Pretty Mary," p. 18
    "I See a Girl," p. 19
    "Blue, Blue," p. 20

- Record: Children's Record Guild "Little Red Wagon," #1004

Snack or lunch

- Colorful foods can be served (slices of fruits or vegetables, juices of different colors).
- The children can help make colored frosting and then spread it on crackers or cookies. Decorating the iced cookies provides them with another color experience.

Outside activities

- Introduce a traffic signal for use with wagons, tricycles, and pedestrians.
- Help the children learn what the different colors mean.

Books Available Throughout the Day

- Curry, Nancy. *An Apple Is Red.* Glendale, Calif.: Bowmar, 1967.
- Duvoisin, Roger. *The House of Four Seasons.* New York: Lothrop, Lee and Shepard, 1956.
- Eicke, Edna. *What's Your Name?* New York: Windmill Books, 1968.
- Emberley, Ed. *Green Says Go.* Boston: Little, Brown and Co., 1968.
- Gottlieb, Suzanne. *What Is Red?* New York: Lothrop, Lee and Shepard, 1961.
- Ipcar, Dahlov. *Black and White.* New York: Alfred A. Knopf, 1963.
- Jaynes, Ruth. *My Tricycle and I.* Glendale, Calif.: Bowmar, 1968.
- McGovern, Ann. *Black Is Beautiful.* New York: Four Winds Press, 1969.
- O'Neill, Mary. *Hailstones & Halibut Bones.* Garden City, N.Y.: Doubleday and Co.
- Radlauer, Ruth and Ed. *Colors.* Glendale, Calif.: Bowmar, 1968.
- Reiss, John J. *Colors.* Englewood Cliffs, N.J.: Bradbury Press, 1969.
- Rossetti, Christina. *What Is Pink?* New York: Macmillan Co., 1971.
- Schlein, Miriam. *Little Red Nose.* New York: Abelard-Schuman, 1955.
- Tresselt, Alvin. *Autumn Harvest.* New York: Lothrop, Lee and Shepard, 1955.
- Zolotow, Charlotte. *One Step, Two . . .* New York: Lothrop, Lee and Shepard, 1955.

Suggested Original Stories

"We're Going to Paint"

A story with this title can take on any of a number of directions. Let's look at just two:

- Suppose a family is going to move into a new house or paint the inside or outside of their present one. Have the family members help decide on the colors. Tell what color each member prefers and why. Then tell about their trip to the paint store and how they finally decide on the color(s).
- Relate a story about a child helping to build or repair something (toy, furniture) and then painting it. He could have some very delightful experiences.

"A Birthday Present"

Tell a story about a child selecting an article of clothing or a toy for his birthday and the reasoning process he goes through to finally decide on a color.

"Each Day a Different Color"

Use a flannel board story about a child wearing a different color of clothing each day and selecting food to match it. You can use all of the primary and secondary colors plus white or multicolors. Involve the children in thinking about a color and food to match it. This can be lots of fun because the children are actively involved.

Further Topics

- I Learn about Color in Seasons.
- I Learn about Color and Temperature (red/warm, blue/cold).
- I Learn about Color Changes in Nature (ripening of fruits, leaves, and blossoms).
- Different Colors Make Me Feel Different Ways.

Chapter 5

Theme 3: Books Help Me Learn (pp. 129-133)

General Suggestions

- Listen to the children to find out what is important to them. Encourage their endeavors but also introduce new ideas as the children seem ready.
- Here is a resource book for teachers on this topic:

Engel, Rose C. *Language Motivating Experiences for Young Children.* Van Nuys, Calif.: DFA Publishing, 1969.

Chapter 6

Theme 1: It Takes Parts (pp. 142-150)

Suggested Verbalization or Ideas

It takes parts to make a whole object. Different pieces that go together are called parts. When all the pieces or parts are put together, they make one object, called a whole object. This whole object has a name different from the names of the parts. State the parts and let the children name the whole object. (The name of the object in parentheses is in many cases only one of several possibilities.)

It takes parts and a frame to make a (puzzle).
It takes pages and a cover to make a (book).
It takes legs, a seat, and a back to make a (chair).
It takes a handle and a scoop to make a (shovel).
It takes two fronts, a back, two sleeves, and a fastener to make a (coat).
It takes a shaft, lead, and an eraser, to make a (pencil).
It takes a handle and a head to make a (hammer).
It takes a handle and a blade to make a (knife).
It takes a handle and tines to make a (fork).
It takes a handle, a head, and bristles to make a (brush).
It takes a container, handles, water, a plug, and a drain to make a (sink).
It takes paint and a brush, crayons, scissors, paste, and paper to make a (picture).
It takes a shell, a white, and a yolk to make an (egg).
It takes roots, a trunk, branches, and leaves to make a (tree).
It takes a peeling, flesh, a core, seeds, and a stem to make an (apple).
It takes apples, sugar, spices, and water to make (applesauce).
It takes a body, a motor, doors, seats, wheels, and a money box to make a (bus).
It takes a body, wings, a tail, a motor, seats, a door, windows, and wheels to make an (airplane).
It takes a tail, scales, fins, a body, and a head to make a (fish).
It takes a large piece of wood, a knob, and a lock to make a (door).
It takes a roof, walls, doors, windows, and a chimney to make a (house).
It takes wheels, a body, a tongue, and a handle to make a (wagon).
It takes a sole, a heel, a toe, a body, a tongue, and laces to make a (shoe: oxford).

It takes a handle and a blade with sharp teeth to make a (saw).
It takes a handle and teeth to make a (comb).
It takes lips, gums, a tongue, and teeth to make a (mouth).
It takes a face, a skull, hair, and ears to make a (head).
It takes a head, a neck, a trunk, arms, hands, legs, and feet to make a (body).
It takes a face, hands, and numbers to make a (clock).

Note: The above information is provided to give you an idea of how you can use parts of objects, combine them, and make a whole object. Using the real object is much more meaningful to children than showing pictures or just talking about the objects. You should select objects from the familiar environment of the child and then move to lesser known or unknown objects in order to help the child increase his learning.

Also in the above information are several examples of the same words being used in different objects and of how you can start with objects with few parts and move to objects having more parts.

Further Topics

● My Body Works for Me (*see* Theme 2, pp. 27-35).
● My Hands and Arms Are Useful (*see* Theme 3, pp. 35-40).
● We're a Family (*see* Theme 1, pp. 57-62).
● Transportation.
● Food: can easily be broken down into many smaller units—the basic four food groups and then categories within each group: fruit, vegetables—roots that we eat (carrots, turnips, radishes, potatoes), stems that we eat (asparagus, broccoli), products that grow on vines (peas, beans, tomatoes), those that grow on stalks (corn, celery), different coverings on fruit and vegetables, and many more (*see* Theme 2, Plants Provide Things for Me, pp. 93-99).
● Animals (domestic, wild)—where they live, what they eat, the kinds of coverings they have (fur, hair, feathers). (See Theme 1, Farm Animals Interest Me, pp. 87-93).
● I Learn about My Community (topography, landmarks, different community helpers, including the policeman). (*See* Theme 3, Many People Live in My Community, pp. 67-72 and Theme 4, The Policeman Helps Me, pp. 72-78).
● I Learn about Clothing (different seasons, different pieces of apparel, different fabrics).
● Color (*see* Theme 2, Give Me Color, pp. 121-129).

Actually, you can use any topic encompassing smaller subgroups and should think of those that will be especially meaningful to this group of children.

Chapter 6

Theme 2: I Learn About Classification (pp. 150-154)

General Suggestions

Additional Aids and Further Topics are not itemized here. So many are possible. Here's a chance to exercise your own imagination.

For valuable supplementary information on the subject of classification, see *A Teacher's Guide to Cognitive Tasks for Preschool* by Owen W. Cahoon (Provo, Utah: Brigham Young University Press, 1974).

BIBLIOGRAPHY

WORKS CITED

Arbuthnot, May H. *Children and Books.* Chicago: Scott, Foresman and Co., 1972.

Beadle, Muriel. *A Child's Mind.* Garden City, N.Y.: Doubleday and Co., 1971.

Bloom, Benjamin S. *Stability and Change in Human Characteristics.* New York: John Wiley and Sons, 1964.

Bruner, Jerome S. *The Process of Education.* Cambridge: Harvard University Press, 1960.

Gagné, Robert M. *The Conditions of Learning.* New York: Holt, Rinehart and Winston, 1970.

Holt, John. *How Children Learn.* New York: Dell Publishing Co., 1967.

Landreth, Catherine. *Preschool Learning and Teaching.* New York: Harper and Row, 1972.

Mager, Robert F. *Developing Attitude toward Learning.* Palo Alto, Calif.: Fearon Publishers, 1968.

Piaget, Jean. *Play, Dreams, and Imitation in Childhood.* New York: W. W. Norton and Co., 1962.

——————. *Psychology of Intelligence.* Translated by H. Weaver. New York: Basic Books, 1969.

Read, Katherine H. *The Nursery School.* Philadelphia: W. B. Saunders, 1971.

WORKS NOT CITED

Child Development Texts

Hurlock, Elizabeth B. *Child Development.* New York: McGraw-Hill Book Co., 1972.

Kennedy, Wallace A. *Child Psychology.* Englewood Cliffs, N.J.: Prentice-Hall, 1971.

Stone, L. Joseph, and Joseph Church. *Childhood and Adolescence.* New York: Random House, 1973.

Group Programs for Young Children

Croft, D. J., and Robert D. Hess. *An Activities Handbook for Teachers of Young Children.* Boston: Houghton Mifflin Co., 1972.

Hess, Robert D., and Doreen J. Croft. *Teachers of Young Children.* Boston: Houghton Mifflin Co., 1972.

Hilderbrand, Verna. *Introduction to Early Childhood Education.* New York: Macmillan Co., 1971.

Leeper, Sarah H., Ruth J. Dales, Dora S. Skipper, and Ralph L. Witherspoon. *Good Schools for Young Children.* New York: Macmillan Co., 1968.

Nixon, Ruth H., and Clifford L. Nixon. *Introduction to Early Childhood Education.* New York: Random House, 1971.

Spodek, Bernard. *Teaching in the Early Years.* Englewood Cliffs, N. J.: Prentice-Hall, 1972.

Taylor, Barbara J. *A Child Goes Forth.* Provo, Utah: Brigham Young University Press, 1970.

Todd, Vivian E., and Helen Heffernan. *The Years Before School.* New York: Macmillan Co., 1970.

Vance, Barbara J. *Teaching the Prekindergarten Child.* Monterey, Calif.: Brooks/Cole Publishing Co., 1973.

INDEX

179